More Praise for *The G*

"Frank Thomas has gathered in
that are critical to the preaching
disconnected. From these he has orchestrated a long overdue but utterly
necessary conversation. *The God of the Dangerous Sermon* and its two companion books will raise up the next wave of preachers who simultaneously
nurture faith communities and bear witness to the God of justice we know
in the face of Jesus Christ."

    —Gregory V. Palmer, resident bishop, Ohio West Episcopal Area, The
United Methodist Church

"Warning to preachers: Do not open this book by Frank Thomas unless
you are ready to be changed. No one lays out both the promise and perils
of preaching with such clarity and compassion. I know I do not live up
to the call of the God of the Dangerous sermon every single Sunday, but
Frank Thomas sure makes me want to. Great teachers and preachers will
do that."

    —Lillian Daniel, senior pastor, First Congregational Church,
Dubuque, IA; author, *Tired of Apologizing for a Church I Don't Belong To*

"This powerful book reminds us that all religion is not inherently good.
It also helps preachers discern if they're serving a tribal god or the living,
loquacious God who 'slants' toward the poor and dispossessed, and who
insists on responding with resurrection to the crosses we build."

    —Jason Micheli, head pastor, Annandale United Methodist Church,
Annandale, VA; author, blogger, and podcaster

"Thomas's work in *How to Preach a Dangerous Sermon* is intentional, detailed, and unrelenting. The brilliant construction of his manuscript in
its three parts takes us on a journey from the classroom to the halls of
history to our front doors and presents a compelling argument for today's
theologians. The tension and examination in his writing makes this work
brilliant."

    —Ron Bell, lead pastor, Camphor United Methodist Church, St.
Paul, MN

"Thomas invites us to reflect deeply and act courageously even when it's dangerous. This book is timely and important for every theologian and practitioner."

—Lia McIntosh, program officer in education, Ewing Marion Kauffman Foundation; certified executive coach, consultant, trainer, speaker; author, *Church/School/Community: Forging Partnerships to Change the World* from Abingdon Press

"Frank Thomas boldly and passionately reminds preachers that our rhetoric reveals our God. With dexterous and definitive argument, he compels us to be accountable for the God behind our rhetoric. Rhetoric can lift up or destroy, offer liberation or maintain the systemic sin of racism. The God of the dangerous sermon revealed in this book calls us to our inherent responsibility for preaching with moral imagination shaped by love and justice."

—Karoline M. Lewis, Marbury E. Anderson Chair of Biblical Preaching, professor of biblical preaching, and director of the Doctor of Ministry in Biblical Preaching, Luther Seminary, St. Paul, MN; program director, Festival of Homiletics; author, *Embody: Five Keys to Leading with Integrity* from Abingdon Press

"Readers who want to advance the conversation about African American preaching will find deep satisfaction in this enlightening text by a celebrated leader in the homiletics guild. This third installment in Thomas's trilogy is as vibrant and memorable as the companion books and serves as a vital resource for anyone who seeks to preach substantive sermons. *The God of the Dangerous Sermon* offers a lively analysis of the union between theology and rhetoric. Absorbing and eye-opening!"

—Donyelle McCray, associate professor of homiletics, Yale Divinity School, New Haven, CT

FRANK A. THOMAS
Foreword by Will Willimon

THE GOD
OF THE
DANGEROUS
SERMON

Abingdon Press™

Nashville

THE GOD OF THE DANGEROUS SERMON

Copyright © 2021 by Abingdon Press

All rights reserved.

ISBN: 9781791020224

Library of Congress Control Number: 2021946023

21 22 23 24 25 26 27 28 29 30 31—10 9 8 7 6 5 4 3 2 1

MANUFACTURED IN THE UNITED STATES OF AMERICA

To the memory of
John "Frank" Thomas
October 6, 1934–January 6, 2021

This book is dedicated to the continuing legacy of John "Frank" Thomas, my dad,
who introduced me to the moral vision of the God of the Dangerous Sermon,
the only God he could serve.

Dad, I thought we had years to go yet. With the diagnosis of stage-four cancer, I realized
that we only had weeks. When the treatments did not stop the growth, we only had days.
When you came home for your final days of care, we only had minutes. When I saw you
lying in bed, I knew only seconds. I asked God to let you die easy. God sent death as a
friend. And then you were gone. I heard you shout salvation in your flight.
We still have eternal time together—soon. Thank you for being my dad.
I pray eternal rest as an ancestor in God's perpetual light.

To the memory of
195,000 members of the United States Colored Infantry,
37,000 of whom died in the Civil War.

See, there above the center, where the flag is waving bright,
We are going out of slavery; we're bound for freedom's light;
We mean to show Jeff Davis how the Africans can fight,
As we go marching on!

CONTENTS

CONTENTS

Shortly after police shot unarmed Jordan Edwards in the back of his head while he was a passenger in a car in Texas, Frank A. Thomas preached a sermon from Lamentations 3 in Duke University Chapel, on August 13, 2017. That Sunday Frank's sermon was delivered in his usual soft-spoken tone but packed a powerful wallop. He gave our congregation maximum opportunity to join him on that daring, risky path toward the Savior who dares to walk toward us. While pulling no punches, Frank beguiled the congregation (nearly all of whom look like me) into consideration that God may have created them to be better than they were bred to be and expected more out of them than white-collar, respectable Trumpism. An unforgettable performance of unsafe gospel preaching.

The next year I read the first of Frank's "dangerous sermon" books. Frank's deep theological commitments have led him to think extensively about America's racist white supremacy sin. And yet he delivers tough truth to readers in a manner that is measured and thoughtful, so much so that we are not blown away by it. I'd rather have Frank convict me of my sin than just about any preacher I know, which tells you a lot about his gracious preaching.

In this, the third in the series of his dangerous but life-giving books, Frank explores preaching as a theological/rhetorical activity. He celebrates the way preachers, particularly in the Black church, have utilized a wide array of stirring rhetorical devices to get the truth about God out to their listeners. At the same time Frank adeptly shows how the rhetoric they used was theologically based, disciplined, and driven.

I, who have been known to decry contemporary homiletics' infatuation with rhetoric, have now been appropriately schooled by Frank A.

Thomas. We have a God who, if scripture be believed, turns toward us through a dazzling array of rhetorical forms and who authorizes God's preachers to do the same.

I'll not forget Frank's analysis of Lincoln's Second Inaugural Address, showing the strengths and weakness of Lincoln's speech, demonstrating how the rhetoric used shows both Lincoln's growth in understanding the sin of American racism and that our ways of speaking can betray the very truth we want to communicate.

With malice toward none, with charity for all, Frank is able to tell the tough truth many of us are reluctant to hear. This book, like Frank's sermon that I heard that day in Duke Chapel, is a demonstration of the fruitfulness of his theological/rhetorical approach to coax us preachers toward more invigorating dangerous sermons. For those of us who are called by God to summon the guts to preach the gospel that not all want to hear, Frank's fresh introduction to the God of the dangerous sermon is encouraging and enlivening. Go ahead, live dangerously, preach!

I predict that this book will change the way you listen for God in the sermon and the way you handle the word of God who is determined, in sermons, to handle us.

Will Willimon

Will Willimon is Professor of the Practice of Christian Ministry at Duke Divinity School, a United Methodist bishop, retired, and author of *Preachers Dare: Speaking for God.*

Follow this link to view the sermon preached by Frank A. Thomas at Duke University Chapel on August 13, 2017: https://www.youtube.com /watch?v=lG6rmDJ2-hs.

Introduction

It is not enough to limit your love to your own nation, to your own group. You must respond with love even to those outside of it. . . . This concept enables people to live together, not as nations, but as the human race.

—Clarence Jordan

*T*he *God of the Dangerous Sermon* is the final installment in an unanticipated and unplanned trilogy. It began with *How to Preach a Dangerous Sermon* (2018), where I raised questions about the limits of moral imagination in both American culture and especially the American Christian church. I suggested dangerous sermons were based in the preacher's moral imagination that upends and challenges the dominant moral hierarchy and the resulting misallocation of freedom, resources, assets, and legitimacy, whereby people at the top are considered deserving "winners" and people at the bottom are miserable "takers" and "losers." The response to the book was overwhelming and almost uniformly the same. Many readers wanted more clarification on exactly what a dangerous sermon was, and, if they preached one, how they could survive (remain employed).

Based upon this feedback, I was pushed to write the second book in the trilogy, *Surviving a Dangerous Sermon* (2020), where I responded to readers' concerns of clarification of a dangerous sermon and suggestions on how to survive the preaching of one. I also presented Andre Resner's concept of "working gospel" and George Lakoff's theory of the unconscious moral worldview to give preachers specific tools to: (1) think deeply and carefully about their own moral worldview, (2) understand the moral worldview(s) in the audience(s) to whom they preach, and (3) predicated on the first two, skillfully craft a sermon that has the best chance to reach multiple moral worldviews, while accounting for the possibility that some or all of the congregation might disagree with the preacher.

In continuing reflection upon moral imagination and the content articulated in the first two books, and a generous push from an important critique of my earlier work by distinguished homiletics professor Cleophus J. LaRue, the third book in the trilogy, *The God of the Dangerous Sermon*, became clear and compelling to write. In his *Re-thinking Celebration: From Rhetoric to Praise in African American Preaching*, LaRue argued that Henry H. Mitchell and myself, in promoting celebration as a chief aspect of African American preaching, offered a "quasi-theological definition of celebration" and have a misplaced importance on "evocative rhetoric."[1] LaRue argues that the Mitchell/Thomas definition of celebration is devoid of theological content, a "merely rhetorical understanding" that causes preachers to work harder on the end as opposed to the substantive beginning and middle of their sermons.

My homiletical project has broadened, and hopefully deepened, since the writing of my first preaching book in 1997 (updated in 2014), *They Like to Never Quit Praisin' God: The Role of Celebration in Preaching*. Beginning with *Introduction to the Practice of African American Preaching* (2016), the primary vision for my homiletical work has been to balance the inherent theological and rhetorical components in the African American preaching event and to treat celebration as an intrinsic part of that balance. As Robert Reid suggests, it is clear that theology and rhetoric are dance partners in preaching, though theology is the lead partner and rhetoric the complementary partner.[2] Many readers will know that in partner dances the basic choreography involves two people moving simultaneously in coordinated fashion. Each partner has their own dance frame, and yet when both frames combine, it makes for an aesthetic of beauty,

---

1. Cleophus J. LaRue, *Re-thinking Celebration: From Rhetoric to Praise in African American Preaching* (Louisville: Westminster John Knox, 2016), xiv.

2. Robert Reid states, "The Divine-human dance is always afoot in preaching; theology must lead, but homiletics still needs to know what its dance partner (rhetoric) is thinking and how to keep from tripping over the steps it takes." See Robert Stephen Reid, "Homiletics Dancing at the Edge of Rhetoric," presented at the Academy of Homiletics, University of Dubuque, December 2006, 10.

flow, movement, power, and synergy neither partner could have created alone. The same is true with theology and rhetoric. Theology has its own logical frame as the leader of the sermonic dance, and so does rhetoric as the following partner. The beauty, movement, flow, power, and symmetry of African American preaching is uniquely possible because African American preaching is fundamentally a theological and rhetorical act.

While the dance analogy is useful for understanding, I realized that I had not gone beyond it to explicitly and consistently clarify the theological vision that informs my use of rhetoric. I really was not clear on the relationship between the theological and rhetorical, had not explained my use of the term "sacred rhetoric," and, in sum total, had neglected to carefully explicate the underpinnings of my rhetorical theology. My hope is to accomplish these goals herein.

What might not be obvious to the casual reader is that in homiletical circles there has historically been a mixed relationship between theology and rhetoric—a checkered relationship between the two, starting in the early church. For a review of the historical relationship between theology and rhetoric, please see "The Historical Relationship between Homiletics and Rhetoric" in *Introduction to the Practice of African American Preaching*.[3]

My attempt herein is to develop a rhetorical theology or a theology of rhetorical inclusion that functions in a complementary relationship with theology as evidenced in African American preaching. From my section in *Introduction to the Practice of African American Preaching*, I agree with Wayne Booth's comment that rhetoric and religion are essentially wedded, and I am responding to his call for "a constructive theology that stops toying with needing to emulate modernity's rationalism or to hide its discourse in tiny enclaves within divinity schools."[4] I attempt, as David Cunningham says, "a theology that refuses to be embarrassed by the fact that its central claims are rhetorically established."[5] I follow Herbert

---

3. Frank A. Thomas, *Introduction to the Practice of African American Preaching* (Nashville: Abingdon Press, 2016), 56–69.

4. Lucy Lind Hogan and Robert Reid, *Connecting with the Congregation: Rhetoric and the Art of Preaching* (Nashville: Abingdon Press, 1999), 17.

5. David Cunningham, *Faithful Persuasion: In Aid of a Rhetoric of Christian Theology* (South Bend, IN: University of Notre Dame Press, 1991).

Simons's argument and make the rhetorical turn. Simons and his colleagues openly acknowledge that knowledge is socially constructed and, therefore, rhetorically rather than logically derived. The turn involves the recognition by many scholars across all disciplines that reason is fundamentally rhetorical; therefore, inquiry as argument and scholarship in the human sciences is basically a rhetorical enterprise of argument-making. The rhetorical turn is "the recognition that no body of inquiry can escape the fact that it conducts its talk and research by way of words and persuasion."[6] In preaching, this means that even divinely revealed truth must be rhetorically contextualized in order to be received by the hearers. Cunningham is correct that all Christian theology is reasoning conducted by means of persuasive argument. I would like to articulate several features of rhetorical theology.

Characteristics of Rhetorical Theology

Rhetorical theology is not singularly categorized by systematic theology as defined by the usual norms of the traditional Eurocentric canon. Rhetorical theology is a lived and experience-based theology, a liberation theology, seeking expressions of faith outside the normative construct of theology as historically delineated by the theological academy. Though heavily influenced by theological and rhetorical mentors of the academy, as well as conversation partners inside the local churches and communities, rhetorical theology has several overall important features: (1) it has an aversion to absolutism, (2) its theory arises from practice, (3) it values right behavior over right doctrine, (4) its view of religion is concerned with personal salvation and social transformation, and (5) it encourages tools of social analysis and activism.

---

6. Herbert Simons, ed., *The Rhetorical Turn: Invention and Persuasion in the Conduct of Inquiry* (Chicago: University of Chicago Press, 1990). This is the second of two collections of essays intended to give birth to what is now called the "Rhetoric of Inquiry" movement.

Aversion to Absolutism

A difficulty with some theology or religious belief is the idea that, because religion appeals to or speaks on behalf of the absolute, religion therefore can be absolute. Absolutism is the belief that values, principles, truths, etc. are absolute and not relative, dependent, or changeable, and therefore human beings can know and speak the absolute and unchangeable truth. While I believe that God is absolute, our human understandings of God are socially constructed and often varied. I am nervous about absolutism in all forms, but especially in religious garb because absolutism has been and is capable of some of the most despicable forms of hypocrisy, violence, pretension, and evil, all in the name of and with the theoretical sanction of the divine will. Far too many believe that their cause is just, and they exclude any possibility of the partiality of their vision.

Rhetorical theology admits that its understanding, revelation, and vision of God is human and partial. With such concepts as "working gospel," rhetorical theology makes room for other understandings of the gospel.[7] Though many read the same biblical text, there are diverse interpretations of the gospel of Jesus Christ. These various interpretations are defined as "working gospels." If we would be open to dialogue and understanding of theological difference, we have the responsibility to articulate our working gospel and listen to other interpretations that might be different. Rhetorical theology makes clear room for the fact that when we say "gospel" of Jesus Christ, we do not all mean the same thing. We would do well in dialogue about "gospel" to say and clarify what we mean.

One of my major rhetorical mentors, Michael Charles Leff, taught that it is better to state your "preferred definition" rather than attempt to articulate a universal definition meant to include and comprehend everything meant by a term. He argued that, traditionally, the attempt to define something in rational terms centers on a response to a "what is" question. For example, what is theology or what is preaching, or what is rhetoric, for that matter? Leff quotes Richard Whately:

---

7. See Frank A. Thomas, *Surviving a Dangerous Sermon* (Nashville: Abingdon Press, 2020), chapter 1: "The Working Gospel and the Bridge Paradigm," 1–14.

It is a "common error" to suppose that a general term has some real object, properly corresponding to it, independent of our conceptions—that, consequently, some one definition in every case is to be found which will comprehend everything that is rightly designated by that term . . . in fact, it will often happen . . . that competent authority allows "a variation in the definitions employed; none of which perhaps may be charged with error, though none can be framed that will apply to every acceptation of the term."[8]

Leff suggests that a more helpful question is: "What is your preferred definition of preaching?" When we respond to this question, often we will describe the preaching that we prefer or have an affinity with rather than a universal definition meant to comprehend everything that is meant by the term. This removes absolutism and makes room for other interpretations. As I relate in *Surviving a Dangerous Sermon*, my working gospel or preferred definition of the gospel is found in Luke's gospel and the concept of the Prophetic Messiah.[9]

Theory Arises from Practice

Again, Leff was suspicious of abstract theory and taught that theory arises from practice. Theory is developed after reflecting on practice, and then theory is revised through application in practice. The foundation of theory is practice. For Leff, practice had the dual function of theory collapse and theory creation. Based in practice, one develops, creates, rethinks, crashes, and sometimes updates theory. This guards against theology being locked in the ivory tower of the academy and having but a distant connection with the active lives of people and the church and the vagrancies of the culture. For rhetorical theology, the actual practice of the faith is at the center of the rhetorical theological enterprise. Thomas R. Kelly articulates best what rhetorical theology believes: Jesus "is the center and source of action, not the end-point of thought. He is the locus of

---

8. Michael Charles Leff, "Tradition and Agency in Humanistic Rhetoric," 7–24, in Antonio de Velasco, John Angus Campbell, and David Henry, *Rethinking Rhetorical Theory, Criticism, and Pedagogy: The Living Art of Michael C. Leff* (East Lansing: Michigan State University Press, 2016), 473.

9. See my *Surviving a Dangerous Sermon*, chapter 2: "The Mystery of the Gospel and the Prophetic Messiah," 19–30.

commitment, not a problem for debate."[10] Practice comes first in religion, not theory or dogma.

I do not subscribe to the academic view that theory is superior to practice. In much of the academy, there seems to be the subtle and yet ever-present hierarchal view that, for example, systematic theology and Bible are foremost, and practical theology is less than because practice is less rigorous. I believe that scholarship can arise out of practice. In fact, if one does intentional and thoughtful practice, questions will arise that require the tools and skills of scholarship to resolve.

Right Behavior over Right Doctrine

Some scholars have made the designation that religion can generally be defined as either belief or practice. There is orthodoxy (right belief in doctrine) and orthopraxy (emphasis on right practice). While it is possible and highly likely that most religions have aspects of both, specific religions tend to emphasize one or the other. While correct doctrine is important, the main emphasis in rhetorical theology is correct practice.

Another of my major theological mentors, Rabbi Edwin H. Fried-man, taught the concept of right behavior being more important than right belief. On the heels of the religious faithful utilizing holy words from holy writ to justify killing and murder in the name of God, he said continuously that he was far more interested in how adherents behaved with their faith than in what they said about their faith. "I know your faith by how you behave more than by what you say" is a careful maxim of rhetorical theology.

I am sure my agreement with Friedman and slanting toward ortho-praxy has to do with my experience as an African American. Slavery, rac-ism, hatred, abuse, and oppression have all been sanctioned with Chris-tian scripture and theological justifications, both historically and in the contemporary moment. I have heard the finest sermonizing and most lovely pronouncements of pristine theology and read and seen support for some of the most despicable acts of violence, oppression, and hate.

---

10.   Thomas R. Kelly, *A Testament of Devotion* (San Francisco: HarperSanFrancisco, 1941, 1996), 8.

If your behavior is abusive and hateful, regardless of what you say about your theology, I assume that the god that you serve is hateful and abusive. Rhetorical theology discerns the god that you serve by the behavior that you exhibit and not the Bible verses and theology that you espouse.

Personal Salvation and Social Transformation

Christianity has to do with both individual salvation/personal piety and cultural critique/social transformation. Tony Campolo relates that when he was twenty-three years old, Clarence Jordan, of whom we will say much more soon, changed his understanding of evangelism. While many speakers at a conference in Chicago said the usual, claiming the chief role of the church was to bring people into a saving relationship with Jesus, Jordan turned the conference upside down:

> While he emphasized that evangelism includes challenging individuals to yield to Jesus . . . [f]or him, evangelism also involves proclaiming what God is doing in society right now to bring about justice, liberation, and economic well-being for the oppressed. Jordan called people to participate in this revolutionary transformation of the world. He opened the Scriptures and showed us that evangelism is what Jesus said it is: broadcasting the good news that the kingdom of God is breaking loose in human history; that a new social order is being created; and that we all are invited to share in what is happening, . . . to live out this good news by becoming involved in breaking down the barriers of racism, sexism, and social class.[11]

Working for social transformation indeed starts with personal salvation. Personal salvation and transformation must lead to social transformation and the examination of moral hierarchies of cultural dominance. In its simplest form, dominance hierarchy believes that the most moral are at the top of the freedom, resource, and legitimacy food chain and the least moral are at the bottom. The people at the top are "winners" and have authority, assets, and legitimacy, while people at the bottom are deservedly "losers" with limited capacity to share in the resources of freedom, power, and wealth. Dominance hierarchy often functions to explain and justify

---

11. Tony Campolo, foreword, in Clarence Jordan, *Cotton Patch Gospel: Luke and Acts* (Macon, GA: Smyth & Helwys, 2011).

position and rank in the moral order: people on top legitimize their rule based upon "winning," whereas people at the bottom, based upon inferior talent or immoral lifestyle choices, are rightly obligated to follow.

Those at the top of the hierarchy are generally more interested in individual salvation/personal piety because, as Emerson and Smith relate, "those who are successful in the world, those of abundant means, those in positions of power (whether they are aware of this power or not) rarely come to church to have the social and political power altered."[12] A large portion of American religion wants to focus exclusively on individual salvation/personal piety and disregard cultural dominance hierarchies. Rhetorical theology is concerned with the practice of religion at both the individual and the social level, where freedom, resources, assets, and legitimacy are reserved for a few.

Critical Use of Social Analysis

Reinhold Niebuhr, called by Cornel West "the greatest religious intellectual in mid-century America," posits a social analysis of moral hierarchy that reveals and challenges, as West says, "the night side of our undeniable human darkness—the persistence of power, greed, conflict, and coercion beneath the surface of order; the fury of self-righteousness; the apathy of despair; and the need for a genuine hope—without optimism or pessimism."[13] For rhetorical theology, religion is a force for social change and transformation, both as it deconstructs oppressive moral hierarchies and reconstructs moral visions of hope and reconciliation. Allow me to quickly summarize important insights by Niebuhr, indicative of rhetorical theology's use of social analysis, though he will be more thoroughly discussed in conversation with the critique of James Cone in chapter 3.

Niebuhr argued there was a radical difference between moral behavior at the individual level and moral behavior of social groups, families, clans, classes, races, genders, states, or nations, hence the title of one of

---

12. Michael O. Emerson and Christian Smith, *Divided by Faith: Evangelical Religion and the Problem of Race in America* (New York: Oxford University Press, 2000), 164.

13. Cornel West, foreword to Reinhold Niebuhr, *Moral Man and Immoral Society: A Study in Ethics and Politics* (Louisville: Westminster John Knox Press, 2nd ed., 2013), xi.

his most regarded books, *Moral Man and Immoral Society*.[14] For Niebuhr, people promote kindness at the individual level, and yet will support and justify political policies "which a purely individual ethic must find embarrassing."[15] In human groups, logic and reason seem less able to check impulses of self-interest and self-concern. Social groups have "less capacity for self-transcendence, less ability to comprehend the needs of others and therefore more unrestrained egotism than the individuals who compose the group reveal in their personal relationships."[16] Langdon B. Gilkey suggests in his introduction to the 2013 edition of Niebuhr's classic, "there can be, without contradiction, the pious slaveowner, the respectable member of the ruling class or aggressive nation, the 'moral' member of an oppressive race. . . . these persons may appear to be moral as individuals, nonetheless they join with others of their group and act with exceeding self-concern, with oppressive ruthlessness, and devastating destruction."[17] The hypocrisy is so obvious one wonders how it can be morally justified. Niebuhr supplies the answer: morals like honesty, fairness, and truth are for personal relationships; in the matter of groups, self-concern and self-interest, often expressed through demonstrations of power, and sometimes raw and abusive power, is the ethic.

Niebuhr critiques moralists, both religious and secular, who argue that the egoism is being checked by rationality or religiously inspired goodwill and that progressively social harmony will be established. Niebuhr suggests that collective behaviors of self-interest are inherent in human nature and will never be subject to reason or conscience:

> They [the moralists] do not see that the limitations of the human imagination [moral imagination], the easy subservience of reason to prejudice and passion, and the consequential persistence of irrational egoism, particularly in group behavior, makes social conflict an inevitability in human history, probably to its very end.[18]

---

14. Niebuhr, *Moral Man and Immoral Society*.

15. Niebuhr, *Moral Man and Immoral Society*, xxxix.

16. Niebuhr, *Moral Man and Immoral Society*, xviii–xix.

17. Niebuhr, *Moral Man and Immoral Society*, xvii.

18. Niebuhr, *Moral Man and Immoral Society*, xxxiv.

Thus, the relations between groups will always be predominantly political rather than ethical. A relationship will be determined by the proportion of power rather than any moral ethic. Niebuhr says, "No group will be forced from power solely by persuasion, by arguments, academic or legal, nor by the moral right of the just and rightness of the case of the oppressed."[19] That is, group relations will be determined by the proportion of power each group possesses as much as by any rational and moral appraisal of the comparative needs of each group. Langdon B. Gilkey interprets Niebuhr:

> Thus only *power* opposed to ruling groups, challenging them, and even forcing them—a political, economic, or in the last resort, military power— will dislodge them and create a more just situation. Clearly justice is on the side of those with less power and less wealth; but the justice of the power- less victim's cause does not, said Niebuhr, imply that victim's greater virtue. When the proletariat gain supreme power, they may well dominate as the nobility and the bourgeoisie did once.[20]

For Niebuhr, power and domination was part of human nature, and in far too many cases whoever has the power will dominate those who do not.

The bottom line is that the dominant classes at the top of the moral hierarchy, based upon their economic interests, attempt to maintain their privilege in all aspects of society, often bending the government and cul- ture to their will. Niebuhr quotes Sir Arthur Salter:

> The failure of governments is due to the pressure of economic interests upon them rather than to the "limited capacities of human wisdom." Gov- ernment is failing because above all else it has become enmeshed in the tasking of giving discretionary, particularly preferential, privileges to com- petitive industry.[21]

Governments give privilege to those of the highest economic class, evident in the vast amounts of wealth inequality made visible in the last forty years. Wealth has accumulated in fewer and fewer hands and gives even more power and control of politics, government, and society.

---

19. Niebuhr, *Moral Man and Immoral Society*, xvii.

20. Niebuhr, *Moral Man and Immoral Society*, xvii.

21. Niebuhr, *Moral Man and Immoral Society*, xxxiii.

Of course, wealth cannot maintain dominance alone; it requires the support and morale of middle-class and many common people. This morale is created by dogmas, religion, symbols, and emotionally potent over-simplifications. The number of people who have deeply, profoundly, and carefully thought through their moral values, and are therefore able to discriminate between good and evil, is very small. In significant parts of the country, regardless of the facts, many people blindly follow the opinion of leaders. For far too many people, their trusted leader(s) or their families, clans, classes, races, etc. establish truth—that is, what is right and wrong, and who is friend and enemy. Good is what my leader and group does, and evil is what the other side does, regardless of the moral merits of behavior. There are very few cases of people who are self-sacrificing enough, despite their religious belief, to oppose the morality or self-interest of the group. I heard an author say, in the best sense of the word, that those who go against the self-interest of their group(s) based upon a broader and wider vision from their moral imaginations are considered "holy fools." We have so very few holy fools.

Many leaders of the church will not challenge the economic class power-dominant hierarchy arrangement and advocate for social change and transformation. Some argue it is too divisive and not their business to champion social causes, but only to admonish the culture and society to a spirit of fairness and accommodation, which, in effect, defaults to the status quo. Rhetorical theology speaks to the truth that this oppressive moral hierarchy creates devastating suffering for those at the bottom.

Despite my idealism, my lived experience is that Niebuhr is correct in his analysis of individual and group morality. I will say much more later, but I believe that only true religion, in my case Christian faith operating in Christian community, gives me the courage and discipline to extend morality from the individual level to beyond the limits and perspectives of my group. If that extension is not made, then adherents are serving a tribal god. Extending moral and ethical behavior outside of my group is what it means to serve a universal God. Allow me to set forth the summary and the imaginative flow of this book.

Imaginative Flow and Summary of *The God of the Dangerous Sermon*

In the hopes of facilitating ease of reading, I have segmented the book into three sections: (1) Homiletical Theory: Conversation Partners with Rhetorical Theology, (2) Close Readings of a Universal and Tribal God, and (3) The God of the Dangerous Sermon.

Section One: Homiletical Theory: Conversation Partners with Rhetorical Theology

In chapter 1, "A Theological and Rhetorical Homiletic," I specifically articulate my response to Cleophus J. LaRue's critique of my concept of celebration in preaching.[22] LaRue has been tremendously helpful by pushing me to identify more explicitly and consistently the theological vision now at the heart of my homiletical work: the seamless partnership between theology and rhetoric in African American preaching, the development of a "rhetorical theology of preaching."

In chapter 2, "Black Sacred Rhetoric," I turn to the inherent relationship between theology and rhetoric in African American preaching by considering William H. Pipes's analysis of "old time Negro preaching" and its frustration with American democracy and the definition of Black sacred rhetoric offered by professor Isaac Rufus Clark. The chapter closes by surveying the contribution of womanist preachers who center their work on rhetoric and theology in African American preaching, Donna E. Allen's exposition of rhetorical criticism and a womanist homiletic, and Kimberly P. Johnson's womanist rhetoric and womanist preaching.

In the third chapter, "Why Have Some So Much and Others So Little?" I am in dialogue with theological ethics, public theology, anthropology, and Christian realism, all in the attempt to discern how resources are divided up and justified in the name of God. I simply want to know why some have so much and others have so little, and these "conversation partners" help me to understand this vital question to my rhetorical

---

22. LaRue, *Re-thinking Celebration.*

13

theology. The work of Andre E. Johnson on James Cone, definition and characteristics of public theology by Sebastian Kim and Katie Day, Roger Sanjek on the 1400s global racial hierarchy still omnipresent today, the Christian realism of Reinhold Niebuhr, James Cone's critique of Niebuhr, as well as a critique of Cone offer rich reflections of critical analysis as to why the haves have and the have-nots have not.

Section Two: Close Readings of a Universal and Tribal God

Chapter 4, "Abraham Lincoln's Moral Imagination: Slavery, Race, and Religion in the Second Inaugural Address," identifies Lincoln's vision of a universal God through the tools of rhetorical criticism and the methodology of close reading. The form of the Second Inaugural was that of a sermon to the nation in the longstanding tradition of the American jeremiad.[23] In the attempt to keep the Union together and save democracy, Lincoln developed, not a cultural dominance hierarchy to announce the North had won and the South, based upon losing the war, was to be punished and subservient, but a universal God that was not on the "side" of either the North or the South. According to Lincoln, the universal God punished both North and South for their contribution, complicity, and collusion in the sin of slavery. Lincoln's address is a paradigmatic example of the concept of a universal God that extends a moral ethic to all. The Second Inaugural was, according to my earlier definition of upending and challenging the dominant moral hierarchy, a dangerous sermon. Lincoln was declaring and appealing to the God of the Dangerous Sermon.

In chapter 5, "White Christian Nationalism, Whiteness, and the Rhetorical Construction of Tribal Gods," I look carefully at President Donald J. Trump's "performance" of whiteness and its theological worldview and appeal in a representative speech of his rhetoric. I closely and critically

---

23. For more information on the tradition of the American and African American jeremiad, see Frank A. Thomas, *American Dream 2.0: A Christian Way Out of the Great Recession* (Nashville: Abingdon Press, 2012). The American jeremiad was a spoken or preached public ritual designed to join social criticism to spiritual renewal calling the nation back to covenant with God. It reminded America of its divine mission established by John Winthrop in 1630. Winthrop, in a sermon at sea aboard the *Arabella*, paraphrased Matthew 5:14 to crystallize New England's mission: "we must consider that we shall be a city upon a hill. The eyes of all people are upon us."

explore the tribal God underneath Trump's rhetoric by examining the white Christian nationalism that provided the spiritual and ideological justification for support of the presidency of Donald J. Trump, particularly from white evangelicals, and also others in the Roman Catholic church and Black church. The bottom line is that in Trump's Rose Garden speech of June 1, 2020, and the subsequent jaunt to St. John's Episcopal Church, we discern the rhetorical construction of a tribal god.

Section Three: The God of the Dangerous Sermon

In the final section and chapter 6, I lay out critical points of rhetorical theology—not in the form and expectations of a systematic theology, but in light of our critical question, why do some have so much and so many have so little? First, I briefly recap my working gospel of the "Prophetic Messiah" in order to clearly demonstrate Jesus's adherence to a universal rather than a tribal God. Second, following Jesus in Luke 4, I give characteristics of the universal God. While a tribal god leads to and condones violence, intimidation, theft, and assault, real and rhetorical, the universal God of the dangerous sermon presents judgment and healing to the entire human community. Third, I specifically discuss several theological questions that were raised and linger from previous chapters in the struggle for racial equality, such as Frederick Douglass's analysis of Lincoln's Second Inaugural that too much forgiveness led to too much acceptance. In other words, what is the relationship between forgiveness and accountability? Fourth, at the end of the Lincoln chapter, I quote Stephen Sondheim from his play *Assassins,* where he raises the question of changing the world by pulling a trigger on a gun with one's "little finger." Is there an alternative to the theological claim of power to change the world because one has a gun and uses "one's little finger"? Finally, are there any possibilities of moral imagination outside of the global racial paradigm? Henceforth, will humanity always be trapped in the 1400s global racial paradigm, or are there other possibilities? I want to discuss the reality and role of the church led by the Spirit of God presenting a vision of a new humanity outside the racial paradigm.

All of us as human beings have a conscious and unconscious moral worldview that directly shapes our moral imagination, which in turn shapes our theology, the rhetoric of our theology and sermons, and then finally our moral behavior in the world. Rhetorical theology discerns our moral imagination and theology through sermons and speeches as a window into our observable behavior in the world, especially to those who are not of our tribe or our group. If our behavior in the world is racist, hateful, and oppressive, then it follows that the god of our moral imagination is racist, hateful, and oppressive. If so, despite what we proclaim in our theology, we are, in fact, serving a tribal god. Every sermon, based in the preacher's moral imagination, has a theology, and a god of that theology behind it. The tribal god is the god of cultural purity, racial and ethnic exclusion, racist tropes, demonization of opponents, apocalyptic claims, authoritarianism, and religious indignation. Our hope is to discern tribal gods from the universal God.

One of my practices, in as many books as is feasible, is to bring to remembrance profound witnesses to truth, freedom, and liberation who have gone on to be with the ancestors. In *How to Preach a Dangerous Sermon*, we remembered Prathia Hall; thankfully now, the work of Courtney Pace is helping another generation to become acquainted with her "freedom faith."[24] In this volume, I remember and remind the church of Clarence Jordan, who formed the Koinonia Farm, a community that served the God of the Dangerous Sermon. His words will be featured in several places throughout this book.

Clarence Jordan Remembered

Jordan was born in Talbotton, Georgia. Since his youth, he had been troubled by the vast racial and economic injustice in his community, and graduated with a degree in agriculture from the University of Georgia with the intent to help sharecroppers. He gained the insight that poverty was economic and spiritual, and in response attended Southern Baptist Theological Seminary in Louisville, Kentucky, receiving a PhD in Greek New Testament in 1938 and becoming ordained as a Southern Baptist minister. In 1942, the Jordans and another couple, Martin and Mabel

---

24. Courtney Pace, *Freedom Faith: The Womanist Vision of Prathia Hall* (Athens: University of Georgia Press, 2019).

England, and their families moved to a 440-acre tract of farmland near Americus, Georgia, to create an interracial, Christian farming community. They called it Koinonia (κοινωνία), meaning *communion* or *fellowship*, which in Acts 2:42 is applied to the earliest Christian community. They believed in the equality of all persons, rejection of violence, ecological stewardship, and common ownership of possessions.

In 1956 Jordan was approached by African American students for help getting into classes at the Georgia Business College (for whites) that were unavailable at any of the Negro colleges. Jordan went to the college president with the students and they laid the problem before him. He said that he sympathized with them and hoped something could be worked out. He called in the registrar, who immediately saw that the problem might set off a bomb and so refused to accept the students. Jordan and the group then approached the chairman of the Board of Regents of the university system, who expressed sympathy, but deferred to the board. When Jordan and the students left, there was a large contingency of press and photographers taking pictures and asking questions.

Jordan headed back to Americus and found the governor of Georgia had already inquired of the sheriff what Jordan was up to. Headlines in the Americus paper announced that an Americus man sought to get two Negro students into the university system. Jordan remarks that anonymous and threatening phone calls came. Cars drove by shooting and shot into their roadside market, which was then dynamited, blowing both the top and sides off. Insurance companies cancelled all Koinonia's insurance policies. People began boycotting them and refusing to sell to them. Jordan says, "It is easy to fight an enemy you can meet, hard to fight strangling economic pressure brought against you."[25]

Business after business denied Koinonia their products. The proprietors, despite having long done business with the farm and despite their avowals to be good Baptists and Christians, listened to people say they would not do business with them if they did business with Koinonia. Jordan would ask businesses, "You are facing the same question we are:

---

25. All Jordan quotes taken from "Clarence Jordan Tells the Koinonia Story," speech given November 10, 1956, Fellowship House, Cincinnati, Ohio, audio, https://www.youtube.com/watch?v=2g1Z-v-Tpl0&feature=emb_rel_end.

will you be true to your convictions or will you sell out for your business?" Jordan said he knew he could break the boycott by acquiescing:

> We know how to break this boycott. All we've got to do is get up on the courthouse square and yell "nigger" a few times and holler "white supremacy" and the rounds. We know the language and how to do the business . . . but with us it's a question of whether we will be true to the highest and noblest regardless of the cost ourselves and that's your problem too.

Jordan said he could not find a businessman, a professional man, and only one minister in the county who made the decision for highest and noblest. The lawyers fell in line with the others, even his own brother.

Legal pressure and injunctions were issued against Koinonia. Despite knowing the case was trumped up against them because of Koinonia's "stand on the race question," his brother Bob, a lawyer and Baptist deacon, still refused to take the case. Jordan testifies to the God of the Dangerous Sermon and reports the conversation:

> "Bob, I said, aren't you a Christian." "Yes!" "Don't you follow Jesus?" "Well, yes, up to a point." "Would that point by any means be the cross?" "Yeah, up to the cross." I said, "Bob, I admire your frankness . . . but I seriously question your discipleship. For Jesus said, 'Except a man take up his cross and follow me, he cannot be my disciple.'" . . . But he said, "Clarence, if I want to take that stand I'd lose my home. I'd lose my practice. I'd lose my business." I said, "Yes, I know all that: you would lose the same thing we're having to lose. Then you could come on to Koinonia and join us, for our requirement is that you have nothing." . . . He said, "I'm not prepared to take that stand."

In the final analysis, as Thomas R. Kelly was quoted earlier in this chapter, "Jesus is the locus of commitment, not a problem for debate." All of us who identify as Christians are facing the same question Jordan asked relative to our commitment: will we be true to our convictions or will we sell out? Will we be true to the highest and noblest regardless of the cost to ourselves? This is the call of the God of the Dangerous Sermon, and so many of us, myself included, will *stop at the point of the cross and find ourselves serving a tribal God.*

HOMILETICAL THEORY: CONVERSATION PARTNERS WITH RHETORICAL THEOLOGY

Section One

HOMILETICAL THEORY: CONVERSATION PARTNERS WITH RHETORICAL THEOLOGY

A THEOLOGICAL AND RHETORICAL HOMILETIC

Isaac Rufus Clark's critique of contemporary preaching is a ministerial indictment that much of our preaching has been either light or lying or both, wherein too many of us have slung together some spiritual slop callously or carelessly, late on Saturday night or early on Sunday morning, with the inevitable consequence of parishioners running from church to church, hollering and knocking over benches in search of genuine food for their souls.

—Katie Geneva Cannon

I am honored that distinguished professor Cleophus J. LaRue would give time and attention to the work of Henry H. Mitchell and myself in the area of celebration in preaching. I share with LaRue the deep concern for the effective witness to God's presence and purposes through the gifts of the African American preaching tradition. It is important to critique and carefully scrutinize some of the excesses of this tradition in order that preachers are not guilty of what Isaac Rufus Clark termed "tampering with people's souls."[1] LaRue, in his book *Re-thinking Celebration: From Rhetoric to Praise in African American Preaching,* provides an awesome opportunity to further clarify and define the preaching project that is now my life's work: the seamless partnership between theology and rhetoric in African

---

1. Katie Geneva Cannon, *Teaching Preaching: Isaac Rufus Clark and Black Sacred Rhetoric* (New York: Continuum, 2007), 23.

American preaching.[2] Most scholarship is improved by constructive feedback and critique, and LaRue's assessment and comments have generated a sharper and clearer articulation, hopefully evidenced in this book, of a rhetorical theology of preaching.

Initially the focus of my work was, following Mitchell, to add methodological analysis and practical proscription to Mitchell's concept of celebration.[3] Kenyatta Gilbert, in his seminal work, *The Journey and Promise of African American Preaching*, raised a very fair critique of Mitchell's work, and hence my work.[4] Gilbert argued that, for Mitchell, the distinguishing mark of black preaching is its rhetorical performative structure, what Mitchell labeled, "preaching to the whole person," or "experiential preaching," which is in its most basic form the joining of intellect and emotion in preaching to reach the "intuitive," and marks celebration, particularly in the close of the sermon, as the distinguishing factor of African American preaching. Gilbert defines Mitchell's work as "rhetorical homiletics" or "rhetorical performative homiletics." Gilbert points out two critical concerns of Mitchell's rhetorical performative method. First, it is not always clear that what is being said about God (theology) is at the heart of the creation of the rhetorical experience. Therefore, it is not really clear if the most important thing is the message-bearing task of the preacher (rhetoric), or the word of God (theology).

It took me several years to consider this critique and begin to shape a substantive response. What moved me along the journey were more years of reflection, my doctoral degree in rhetoric itself, and flat out more teaching of preaching and preaching in the pulpit. I began to understand that my preaching project had broadened to address Gilbert's concerns: to balance the theological and rhetorical in African American preaching, and celebration as an inherent part of that balance. My initial articulation of my project was the publication of *Introduction to the Practice of African American Preaching* in 2016, and then *How to Preach a Dangerous Sermon*

2. LaRue, *Re-thinking Celebration*.

3. Frank A. Thomas, *They Like to Never Quit Praisin' God: The Role of Celebration in Preaching* (Cleveland: United Church Press, 1997).

4. Kenyatta R. Gilbert, *The Journey and Promise of African American Preaching* (Minneapolis: Fortress Press, 2011), 22.

in 2018. Then LaRue published *Re-thinking Celebration,* and I saw the need to develop and more clearly articulate the theological side of my rhetorical theology. While writing and publishing *Surviving a Dangerous Sermon* in 2020, I intentionally began to be more expressive of my theology. I explored Andre Resner's concept of "working gospel," Ed Farley's critique of the "bridge paradigm" of contemporary preaching, whether we preach the Bible or the gospel, and, therefore, what then is the relationship between the Bible and the gospel? I expressed my own working gospel, following Luke's revelation and explanation of Jesus as the prophetic messiah based in Luke 4:14-30, a summary of which will be set forth in the final chapter.

With the feedback of graduate students in the PhD Program of African American Preaching and Sacred Rhetoric, particularly Edgar "Trey" Clarke, it became clear that if theology and homiletics was defined from a fairly narrow perspective, such as in the manner of the early church but including Barth, LaRue, and the majority of the field of homiletics in general, my scholarship would never be adequately "theological."[5] The question was not if my homiletical work was adequately theological, but rather what kind of theology undergirds my scholarship? Rhetorical theology undergirds my scholarship, an expression of faith seeking to understand the lived experience of African American preaching outside of normative constructs and boundaries of the practical theological frame. Gilbert, LaRue, and my students have been extremely helpful in pushing me to identify more explicitly and consistently the theological vision that informs my use of rhetoric.

My argument herein is contrary to the binary split between theology and rhetoric offered by the majority in the field of homiletics, including LaRue in *Re-Thinking Celebration.* I want to definitively respond to LaRue's critique that Mitchell and Thomas's concept of celebration in African American preaching is "contrived rhetoric purposely structured into our sermons to guarantee emotional rejoicing at the end."[6] LaRue argues that celebration, as defined by Mitchell and Thomas, is a

---

5. PhD candidate Edgar "Trey" Clarke at Fuller Theological Seminary reflected the core of these thoughts to me in an amazing follow-up email after hearing me lecture in class.

6. LaRue, *Re-Thinking Celebration,* xv.

"quasi-theological" concept based in the "mis-placed importance attached to evocative rhetoric."[7] A summary of LaRue's critique is based in this statement from *Re-thinking Celebration:*

> [C]elebration as a useful rhetorical tool, separate and apart from an understanding of its doxological and liturgical roots, must be critiqued lest the celebratory aspects of black worship and preaching degenerate into meaningless cultural rituals (festivity) that take away from rather than add to the depths of and richness of our worshipful praise that comes for our longed-for encounter with transcendence.[8]

Points of Agreement with LaRue

I find many points of general agreement with LaRue in his discussion of the excesses of celebration in African American sermons. I summarily agree that African American sermons would benefit greatly by ceasing such an exclusive focus on celebrative endings to the diminishment of substance and content. LaRue suggests: "Our emotional rejoicing in worship grows stronger and stronger while our understanding of Scripture and theology seems to grow weaker and weaker. We are emphasizing emotional rejoicing too much and substantive content in our sermons too little."[9]

I lament with LaRue that the effort to leave people "standing up," "shouting," and viscerally emotional at the end of the sermon is an intense pressure in many parts of African American preaching as in no other culture. To this end, audiences can be easily manipulated and in some instances abused. We have far too many preachers more interested in the close than in the entire sermon. We have preachers that will exclusively watch closes of sermons on YouTube, Vimeo, etc. to copy, imitate, and paste celebrations onto sermons to simulate emotions and leave people in an emotional frenzy. It is almost as if the close is more important than

---

7. LaRue, *Re-Thinking Celebration*, xiv.

8. LaRue, *Re-Thinking Celebration*, 19.

9. LaRue, *Re-Thinking Celebration*, ix.

the sermon. Far too many preachers discombobulate the close from the sermon itself, as if the sermon and the entire worship service and liturgical experience is a warmup for the close of the sermon. It is as if the sermon close itself is the chief, premiere, and final dispenser of grace.

I agree with LaRue about this. There have been times when, after hearing in their congregations the preaching of a small number of students to whom I have taught the substantive theological content of the celebrative method, I wonder if my teaching was in vain. I see far too many succumb to the pressure of the vaunted, ritualistic, and overhyped emotional close in the Black church to the sacrifice of theological content and sermon structure. What's even more dangerous, as LaRue comments, is that our excessive celebration can separate congregations from social action and thereby distance people, especially millennials, from the church:

> While we are jumping up and down, shouting, and waving our hands in the air every Sunday during the worship hour, we seem not to notice the growing number of churched and unchurched alike who are becoming powerfully alienated from any form of institutional religion.[10]

There are several more points in LaRue's critique that are solid, sensible, and true. LaRue mentions that celebration as simply a rhetorical tool puts undue pressure on the preacher to close out Sunday's sermon on a highly emotional note, thereby missing lament as an aspect of celebrative preaching. LaRue quotes Otis Moss III concerning the importance of "blues sensibility" and Barbara A. Holmes and Luke Powery as to the importance of contemplation and lament in preaching.[11] I agree that blues sensibility, contemplation, and lament are often normal and healthy aspects of preaching the gospel to the entire range of human experience. The Bible itself includes and addresses every aspect of human experience. I believe that blues sensibility, contemplation, and lament exemplify

---

10. LaRue, *Re-Thinking Celebration*, ix.

11. Otis Moss III, *Blue Note Preaching in a Post-Soul World* (Louisville: Westminster John Knox, 2015); Barbara A. Holmes, *Joy Unspeakable: Contemplative Practices of the Black Church* (Minneapolis: Fortress, 2004); Luke Powery, *Spirit Speech: Lament and Celebration in Preaching* (Nashville: Abingdon Press, 2009).

appropriate emotions and are part of the process of coming to the place of celebration in preaching.

I believe also that there are times when the sermon should leave us in sober reflection and honest pondering as to what God would have us to do or be; when the sermon must challenge us with a call to decisive action resulting from noiseless thought and contemplation; when lament and blues sensibility is a necessary healing balm for the soul, in the language of Howard Thurman, "in quietness and confidence." Such sermons of challenge are entirely as appropriate as visceral and more demonstrative sermons and their responses. Sometimes in the rush to the highly emotive close that seeks to inspire and encourage people, we miss that challenge is a part of spiritual growth. In fact, we can both challenge and inspire. Lament, inward reflection, and contemplation can be as deeply emotive and celebrative as much as outwardly visceral and demonstrative expressions of celebration. Many continue to confuse celebration as a rhetorical trope and style choice at the end of the sermon rather than a theological affirmation of hope that can be reflected in many different rhetorical styles.

We often miss the fact that ideas, inward reflection, and contemplation can be as deeply emotive and celebrative as are outward and demonstrative expressions of celebration. The preaching of Howard Thurman is clear evidence to this truth.[12] Thurman's preaching, and that of many others of the contemplative preaching tradition, makes clear that the celebrative homiletic is broad enough to include many forms and expressions. It is not the style of the close or emotional frenzy that makes the sermon celebrative; it is affirmation of the theological truth of the gospel leading to the natural outpouring of a hopeful, positive mood and emotions. How one celebrates, demonstratively or reflectively, is a stylistic, personal, and cultural choice. What one celebrates is clear: theological hope from the word of God and the good news of the gospel clearly explained to address the contemporary situation. Old preachers, in their homiletic wisdom, would say: "Good meat makes its own gravy." They mean that the celebration naturally flows from presentation of substantive theological content

---

12. A classic example is Howard Thurman's sermon, "Charting the Inward Sea" (1952), on *The Living Wisdom of Howard Thurman: A Visionary for Our Time,* audio CD, Sounds True Session One, Track 4.

and does not therefore have to be concocted, made up, forced, or tacked on. They were warning of the flaws of excessive celebration.

I teach my students that if we are not careful, we will only have one way to judge the work of the Holy Spirit through the sermon in the life of the hearer, that is, if the sermon moves us with visceral outwardly demonstrative positive emotions. This is false, because my experience is that the message of truth delivered by the preacher and the Holy Spirit does not always bring demonstrative positive emotions that result in encouragement and inspiration. I believe the preaching of the gospel is, as Gardner C. Taylor says, "ultimately kind." Sometimes, the Holy Spirit and the truth of God in the sermon make me mad, convict me of my wrong, demand that I repent, force me to swallow my pride, go back and apologize, and thunder clap me out of my silence and lethargy to take an unpopular stand against injustice and oppression. While the gospel is good news, and ultimately kind, sometimes the gospel begins with a difficult and hard critique of my life and behavior and our cultural context, and then presents a redemptive invitation to begin anew.

The indomitable preacher Fred Craddock has an article and audio lecture entitled "Thirteen Ways to End a Sermon."[13] I jokingly remark to my students in preaching class that growing up in the Black church I thought there was only one way to close the sermon—to leave them standing and shouting. When we feel the pressure to close out each sermon on an incredible high, we miss the totality of the shades and nuances of the movement of the Holy Spirit in human experience. *When we get caught in the stylistic stereotype of one genre of close, we do not take up the deepest challenge of finding the appropriate close for this sermon, before these people on this day, given the truth of the word of God in this hour, the uniqueness of our person, and the cultural context in which we find ourselves preaching.* This challenge is one of the most difficult aspects of preaching, and sometimes so difficult that we settle for the canned and the cliché close to mediate and absolve us of this awesome responsibility.

---

13. Fred B. Craddock, "Thirteen Ways to End a Sermon," in *Craddock on the Craft of Preaching*, ed. Lee Sparks and Kathryn Hayes Sparks (St. Louis: Chalice, 2011), 157–168; Fred B. Craddock, "Thirteen Ways to End a Sermon," audio CD, Bell Tower Productions, 2008.

With LaRue, I have noticed that when celebration is divorced from theological content it robs hearers of a deeper connection and experience of God and seems to encourage the congregation to exude a pasted-on, surface, superficial joy, which can often border on frivolous entertainment. There can be a very thin line between gospel preaching and entertainment via the gospel in preaching. I do not mean to insist that preaching must be somber, for there is, as Cicero suggests, an aspect of "delight" in preaching. Cicero is famous for saying, "An eloquent man or woman must speak so as to teach, to delight, and to persuade . . . to teach is a necessity, to delight is a beauty, and to persuade is a triumph."[14] Cicero suggests it is critical to have an aspect of delight and beauty in preaching. It is not a sin to adorn the sermon with beauty in language and theological content, artful presentation, and riveting and gripping attention-holding delivery. Yet on several occasions, I have witnessed the excessive attention to stylized presentation and overhyped delivery and have wondered if what I just witnessed was shallow, light-hearted entertainment. Where the line is, I am not sure, but as preachers we should be mindful of it, lest we sling together "spiritual slop callously or carelessly, . . . with the inevitable consequence of parishioners running from church to church, hollering and knocking over benches in search of genuine food for their souls."[15]

The congregation's response to entertainment can often be choreographed to that of the preacher, and congregation and people are left with a shallow experience of the truth of the gospel. While it is sometimes difficult to judge, because in truth only God knows, a lack of theological content is a sure marker that we are headed in the direction of a motivational speech at best or entertainment at worst. A focus on theological content can be a corrective to pure entertainment in preaching. We can become so predictable and ritualized that the children get to know our "moves." Those of us who grew up in the church are familiar with the children's game of imitating the preacher, the deacons, and sister and brother so-and-so. Back in the day, some older adult would overhear us and tell us to "Stop playing with God." As preachers, we must be careful with gospel

14. Cicero, "On Invention." *The Best Kind of Orator*. Topics, trans. H. M. Hubbell, Cicero Volume II, Loeb Classical Library 386, 1949.

15. Cannon, *Teaching Preaching*, 53.

entertainment in preaching because we could be "playing with God," or again, as Isaac Rufus Clark says, "tampering with people's souls."

I believe, as LaRue suggests, overemphasis on the close can focus too much attention on the preacher and set up tension between "sacramental community and heroic individualism."[16] It can place an overemphasis on the personality and emotive skills of the preacher and overlook character and integrity in preaching. This leads to the temptation of American "celebrity culture" in preaching. Every preaching tradition has practitioners who, because of genius in the demonstration of the tradition, rise and become celebrated and imitated. There will always be preachers who the people hear gladly. There is nothing wrong with this, but I am warning of the temptation of fame in American culture—the attraction, pull, and lure of cash, cameras, and crowds in the preaching of the gospel.

In contradistinction to celebrity culture, sometimes preaching the word of God will not make you popular at all. The Hebrew prophets are evidence, as well as modern-day prophets. Martin Luther King Jr., Prathia Hall, Jeremiah A. Wright Jr., Pauli Murray, William Barber, and others give evidence that preaching prophetic and dangerous sermons will not make one popular, especially with those in positions of power. In *Surviving a Dangerous Sermon*, I suggest that not every sermon should be a dangerous sermon, but every now and then the preacher must move into the realm of challenging and upsetting dominance hierarchies.[17] After everything is said and done, even the preaching of Jesus was not popular in some circles. One need only look at the reception of his preaching at his home synagogue in Luke 4:16–30. They wanted to throw him off the cliff.

In summary, I concur with LaRue that it is high time for substantive critique and candid conversations from African American homileticians and professors of preaching about the excesses in Black preaching. I appreciate LaRue starting off the conversation that I hope many will add to so that our preaching does not tamper with the souls of people. Yet I believe he misinterpreted and misunderstood the Mitchell and Thomas concept of celebration.

---

16. LaRue, *Re-Thinking Celebration*, 23–24.

17. Thomas, *Surviving a Dangerous Sermon*, 134–36.

Points of Disagreement with LaRue

My fundamental disagreement with LaRue is that he misplaces these aforementioned excesses at the close of the sermon squarely at the feet of the celebrative method espoused by Mitchell and myself. LaRue argues that we offer a "quasi-theological definition of celebration" and have a misplaced importance on "evocative rhetoric."[18] He says that the Mitchell/Thomas definition of celebration is devoid of theological content, a "merely rhetorical understanding" that causes preachers to work harder on the end as opposed to the substantive beginning and middle of their sermons. The celebrative method is "evocative rhetoric often masquerading as praise," a "contrived rhetoric," "misguided rhetorical emphasis," simply "a display of well-crafted rhetoric" devoid of theological import.[19] In summary, LaRue argues:

> Mitchell and Thomas have too narrowly defined celebration as word-centered revelry set apart from corporate worship and happening only at the end of the sermon; thus their emphasis is on an animated doxological denouement.[20]

In fact, what LaRue has done in his analysis is to cleave celebration from the connected structure of the sermon. He misunderstands the reality that celebration is connected to the sermon as the result of the overall celebrative structure of the sermon. Based in the oral traditions of Africa and the existential angst of white supremacy in African American life, many African American sermons are situated in the storytelling form progressing from trouble to grace—trouble in the text progresses to life in the gospel that overcomes the trouble with grace, love, hope, and truth.[21] Grace is stronger, and, as Paul Scott Wilson says, "trouble to grace

---

18. LaRue, *Re-Thinking Celebration*, xiv.

19. LaRue, *Re-Thinking Celebration*, 4.

20. LaRue, *Re-Thinking Celebration*, 5.

21. Paul Scott Wilson argues that Milton Crum originates the description of the trouble/grace school, the biggest school in preaching today. Wilson acknowledges African American preaching as a major force in the trouble/grace school. See Paul Scott Wilson, *Preaching and Homiletical Theory* (St. Louis: Chalice, 2004), 101–15.

re-enforces the overall movement of faith: *from* the exodus *to* the promised land, *from* crucifixion *to* the resurrection and glory."[22] The theological and rhetorical sermon structure from trouble to grace that I advocate is situation-complication-resolution-celebration.[23] The celebration is the result of the following structural flow of the sermon:

The preacher describes the situation. Something happening in and around the text is matched by something in and around a contemporary personal/social situation. The preacher creates identification in the listener with the biblical context and the contemporary moment.

The preacher describes the complication. The preacher articulates some existential angst, trouble, or discrepancy in the text and contemporary experience of the audience. A skilled preacher helps the audience to identify with the complication as well.

The preacher describes the resolution to the complication. The resolution of the existential angst is singularly the explication of the Bible text. Theological weight and substance is offered here, the result of exegesis and substantive theological reflection. The focus in the text is what God is doing and saying, or the essence of God's character, based upon what God is doing or saying. The theological content resolves the complication and this is what makes the sermon biblical.

The listener is invited to celebrate in the final movement of the sermon. Because the theological substance resolves the existential angst, the listener is said to experience the good news of the gospel. Celebration is the joyful and ecstatic reinforcement of the theological content that the preacher has already taught the people in the body of the sermon.

22. Wilson, *Preaching and Homiletical Theory,* 98.

23. For more information on structure (situation, complication, resolution, and celebration), see my books *They Like to Never Quit Praisin' God* and *Preaching As Celebration: Digital Lecture Series and Workbook,* rev. ed. (Indianapolis: Hope for Life International, 2018).

LaRue mentions situation-complication-resolution-celebration, but does not fully explicate that the structural movement of the sermon innately leads to celebration as a theological affirmation of God's activity in the text expressed in the preacher's choice of rhetorical style. In the final analysis, my explanation of the celebrative structure is this: "Celebration is the *culmination* of the sermonic design, where a moment is created in which the remembrance of a redemptive past and/or the conviction of a liberated future transforms the events immediately experienced."[24]

As the culmination of the celebration process and design of the sermon, celebration is, therefore, so much more than evocative rhetoric tacked on at the end of the sermon for emotive effect. When the sermon is structured correctly, celebration is the natural and human response to the presented theological good news of the gospel.[25]

At the heart of true celebration is theological substance. Celebration is only possible because of the actions of God or the character of God revealed in the text(s) being preached. It is God who moves, heals, delivers, fixes, announces, judges, proclaims, anoints, appoints, inspires, corrects, and rebukes; it is the action of God that reveals the character of God. The text reveals God, and our preaching and actions are in response to what has been revealed. The theology of God is the source and content of the celebration, though the method of celebration is highly rhetorical, hence the theo-rhetorical nature of African American preaching.

In fairness to LaRue, he does suggest that the fault of excesses in celebration is not the fault of Mitchell and Thomas:

> I am not suggesting that the problems created by our present-day misunderstandings of celebration as useful rhetoric as opposed to worshipful praise are the sole responsibility of Mitchell and Thomas. Transcribed sermons from the eighteenth and nineteenth centuries, along with recorded black sermons from the twentieth century known as race records, will show the

---

24. Thomas, *They Like to Never Quit Praisin' God*, 49.

25. After defining the nature and purpose of African American preaching as helping people experience the assurance of grace (the good news) that is the gospel of Jesus Christ, in a little discussed chapter of *They Like to Never Quit Praisin' God*, I set forth a biblical and theological base for celebration. See "A Theology of Celebrative Preaching," 35-48.

powerful role emotion has played in black preaching long before the publishing careers of either of these men.[26]

I am appreciative of this clarification, and I wish that LaRue had stated it up front, early, and often. The lack of theological substance leading to excesses of celebration in Black preaching began long before Mitchell and Thomas. But given the rhetorical force of LaRue's argument, with phrases for celebration such as "contrived rhetoric," "mis-guided rhetorical emphasis," and "quasi-theological," the assignment of fault can easily be misinterpreted. Perhaps a different choice of adjectives or avoiding the suggestion that it is "mere" rhetoric—given the cultural connotation of rhetoric for many as fluff, words that are not serious and substantive, throw-away verbiage, and even deceptive and misleading language—would have better clarified his point.

The roots of excess in celebration are much deeper than the celebrative method alone. Some of the excesses are in the character and integrity of the preacher. I might even suggest that some excess in celebration might have to do with faulty or nonexistent attempts at biblical exegesis. One of my retired colleagues in preaching, Ronald J. Allen, would frequently highlight to me his concern with the lack of solid biblical exegesis in far too much preaching.

My anecdotal discussion with contemporary preachers makes clear that less emphasis is now placed on traditional exegetical categories, such as using scholarship to get as close as possible to the original intended meaning. I sense that traditional exegesis holds forth in seminary and places of academic training, but when many get to congregational life, their major concern is the exegesis of the congregation or the context over traditional biblical exegesis.

If celebration is focused on the theological substance in the text, but we do less study and have less regard for exegesis and theological interpretation of the text, then it is not hard to conclude that sermon and celebration can be based in exegesis of the congregation rather than exegesis of the text. This can easily lead to the kinds of abuses that LaRue critiques. It might be that we are living in a time when the role of exegesis in preaching

---

26. LaRue, *Re-thinking Celebration*, 27.

is shifting. If so, LaRue and I would concur in calling for a return to theological substance and interpretation.

LaRue posits that Mitchell and Thomas have disembodied celebration from the sermon and set up an evocative and manipulative celebrative emotion. He disembodies celebration from the process of the celebrative design and then attacks it as being "dis-embodied." I run the risk of being redundant, but I want to be clear: I agree with LaRue that some preachers are excessive and cleave celebration from the sermon. This is singularly not the fault of the celebrative method that Mitchell and I teach.

I am deeply appreciative of my mentor Henry H. Mitchell, Kenyatta Gilbert, Cleophus J. LaRue, and my many students who have offered feedback and pushed me to articulate and rhetorically symbolize the theology that is in my soul. It would never have come out without that dialogue. As the Bible says in Proverbs 27:17 (CEV), "Just as iron sharpens iron, friends sharpen the minds of each other."

Chapter 2

BLACK SACRED RHETORIC

His preaching [old-time Negro preacher], for sure, is unique. He must interest his hearers, but he must not mention their most vital problem: white supremacy in the South. Therefore, the Negro minister appeals mainly to the emotions of his audience and leads his hearers to thinking primarily of things of the world which is to come after death, "for God's Got the World in His Hands."

—William H. Pipes

A definitive partnership between theology and rhetoric was forged in the deepest bowels of the African American preaching tradition, once termed "Black sacred rhetoric." Over the whole, African American preaching has believed that preaching is divine and human speech, inherently theological and rhetorical, and grounded in the divine mandate of liberative theology to meet the existential need for justice and liberation, hence the term "Black sacred rhetoric." In this chapter, I explore the African American preaching tradition and its identification of Black sacred rhetoric. Though the term is out of fashion today, the following discussion and historical understanding of it helps ground our discussion of rhetorical theology in centuries of African American preaching.

African American scholars William H. Pipes, Gerald Lamont Thomas, and Isaac Rufus Clark have used frames of both theology and rhetoric to explore the depth and dimensions of Black preaching.[1] Often they apply the Aristotelian rhetorical proofs (ethos, logos, and pathos) and even four of the five canons of rhetoric (invention, disposition, style, and delivery) to the study of Black preaching. I discuss first the work of William H. Pipes on old-time Negro preaching and frustration with American democracy, and then the characterization of the Black sacred rhetoric of Isaac Rufus Clark. Next I turn to Andre E. Johnson to define the Black sacred rhetoric of James Cone. I close by surveying the contemporary contribution of womanist theorists to this discussion of God speech and human speech in African American preaching by way of Donna E. Allen's exposition of rhetorical criticism and a womanist homiletic, and Kimberly P. Johnson's womanist rhetoric and womanist preaching.

William H. Pipes: Old-time Negro Preaching and American Frustration

William H. Pipes, in his book *Say Amen Brother! Old-Time Negro Preaching,* originally published in 1951, uses recordings of seven sermons to study old-time Negro preaching in Macon County, Georgia.[2] Pipes suggests that "old-time and old-fashioned preaching refer to the more emotional preaching of the uneducated Negro ministers (originally of the slavery days), whose preaching is old-time in comparison with the more intellectual and less emotional preaching of the educated Negro of to-day" (first half of the twentieth century).[3] Old-fashioned Negro preaching flourished on big slave plantations and was principally to be found in the "Black Belt, the Southern part of the country possessing thick, dark, and naturally rich soil, where slaves were most profitable and were taken in

---

1.   William H. Pipes and Isaac Rufus Clark are cited extensively. See Gerald Lamont Thomas, *African American Preaching and the Contribution of Dr. Gardner C. Taylor,* Martin Luther King Jr. Memorial Studies in Religion, Culture, and Social Development (New York: Peter Lang, 2004).

2.   William H. Pipes, *Say Amen Brother! Old-Time Negro Preaching: A Study in American Frustration* (Detroit: Wayne State University Press, 1951, rev. 1992).

3.   Pipes, *Say Amen Brother!* 163.

the largest numbers."[4] Pipes states his reason as to why he chose Macon County, Georgia:

> Only in the "Black Belt" do we still have situations that are very close to the Negro's slavery days; the slave plantations with master and slaves have become plantations with landlord and [share]croppers; here alone have the Negro's earliest (old-time) religious practices been kept almost intact.[5]

Pipes makes use of classical rhetorical categories to summarize the characteristics of old-time Negro preaching, utilizing four canons of rhetoric (invention, disposition, style, and delivery). He argues that "the treatment of the Macon County sermons will show that the Negro minister, unknowingly [in academic terms], observes many of the traditions of sacred rhetoric."[6]

Pipes's intriguing subtitle: *Old Time Negro Preaching: A Study in American Frustration* is significant because it is both Pipes's study of the substance of old-time Negro preaching and the quest for Black democratic citizenship in that preaching that unites the theological and rhetorical in the old-fashioned Black sermon. The preacher's choice was force and armed violence or force of speech aimed as principal methods of liberation. Given minority status and American institutional armed force and policing, force or violence, ultimately, was not a practical option for freedom and democracy, though it had been tried in numerous slave rebellions. Marginalized African American formalized a relationship between theology and rhetoric given that persuasion, or adherence of minds, was the only vital option for liberation.

Pipes suggests that the primary challenge of African American people in their difficult and triumphant sojourn in America is white supremacy. As such, he argues the major theological and rhetorical challenge of the old-time Negro preacher:

> His preaching, for sure, is unique. He must interest his hearers, but he must not mention their most vital problem: white supremacy in the South.

---

4. Pipes, *Say Amen Brother!* 163.

5. Pipes, *Say Amen Brother!* 34.

6. Pipes, *Say Amen Brother!* 2.

Therefore, the Negro minister appeals mainly to the emotions of his audience and leads his hearers to thinking primarily of things of the world which is to come after death, "for God's Got the World in His Hands."[7]

First, the basic thrust of what Pipes suggests as "thinking primarily of things of the world which is to come after death," is true for some, and also not true for others. Scholarly evidence reveals that much old-time Negro preaching was nuanced, having shades of the tradition of double meaning contained in the spirituals and a regular part of African American discourse. While speaking to "over yonder," preachers also spoke to concrete liberation realities in the here and now, sometimes in deeply coded language with double meanings.

African American preachers have always had and, in my estimation, always will have, this same challenge of confronting the reality of white supremacy and, by and large, great amounts of racial indifference. Black people have always had to persuade white supremacist America that we were, first, human beings, and then full human beings with equal rights as citizens. Much of the black community has had to rely upon theological belief and substance, that is, God's character and God's activity in the world, to establish dignity and liberation for oppressed people. Black people, who generally saw the Bible as authoritative, have historically derived their sense of humanity and worth from God revealed in the theological substance of the imago dei (the image of God), the Exodus paradigm, the Hebrew prophets, and Jesus. This theology coupled with rhetorical persuasion in its many forms—nonviolent protest, courts, boycotts, black economics, sit-ins, legal remedies, community organizing, voting, speeches and sermons of inspiration, moral suasion, and such—were instruments to petition rights and gain equality. The Black preacher relied upon persuasion and involved rhetorical strategies and tactics to make theological substance practical, implementable, and effective for the comfort, protest, healing, and transformation of the Black community. My argument is Black churches that had a liberation agenda never had the possibility of divorcing theology and rhetoric. Persuasion was a tool of liberation.

---

7. Pipes, *Say Amen Brother!*, 2.

In the theological and rhetorical appeal for liberation, Pipes calls white America to task for denying Blacks' first-class American citizenship and demands that America practice true democracy *for all people* by removing the half-a-century-old concept of separate but equal. Then, Pipes, not to let the Black church off the hook, calls for better Black leadership. He warns that degreed and educated Black educators, ministers, writers, and the like should not delude themselves into thinking that they are the true leaders. Pipes says, "[T]he crying need in improving the Negro masses . . . is for improved Negro leadership."[8]

The truth of Pipes's statement has been and is still relevant: the theological and persuasive task of the African American preacher is to announce and demonstrate God's character and action in the world for liberation (theology) and interest hearers to join God in God's emancipatory work in the world (rhetorical). The preacher speaks to the basic reality that the daily existence of far too many Black people must be lived in an often hostile world dominated by structures of white supremacy, and the responses of many African American preachers for God's liberation and justice were always theological and rhetorical.

The Black Sacred Rhetoric of Isaac Rufus Clark

Isaac Rufus Clark fundamentally links and weds theological and rhetorical traditions together in the use of the term "Black sacred rhetoric."[9] Clark's name is mostly absent from anthologies and publications on Black homiletics despite his sizeable influence on the Black pulpit during his twenty-seven-year tenure (1962–1989) as Fuller E. Callaway Professor of Homiletics at the Interdenominational Theological Center in Atlanta,

---

8. Pipes, *Say Amen Brother!*, 160.

9. Isaac Rufus Clark was an ordained Elder in the African Methodist Episcopal Church. He was awarded the Doctor of Theology degree in systematic theology in 1958 from Boston University, pastored several congregations, and joined the faculty at the Interdenominational Theological Center (ITC) of Atlanta, Georgia, in 1962 where he served as the Fuller E. Callaway Professor of Homiletics until his death in 1989.

Georgia. Clark singled out Katie Geneva Cannon to ensure his distinct homiletical methodology received the critical attention it deserves in the twenty-first century. Subsequently Cannon published *Teaching Preaching: Isaac Rufus Clark and Black Sacred Rhetoric.*[10] Cannon explores Clark's homiletical method and definition of preaching as "holy intellectual inquiry."[11] Much could be said about his homiletical genius, but I would like to focus on Clark's definitive and unapologetic connection of theology and rhetoric in African American homiletics.

In an overall summary of the theological and rhetorical aspects of Clark's homiletic, Cannon says this:

> Clark's language is grounded in a non-negotiable theological mandate: to apply the principles of rhetoric to the particular ends and means of the Christian gospel, for the purpose of liberation, reconciliation, and maturation in the deepest theological sense of the term, so that as professionals of the Word of God, we will never be guilty of unconsciously tampering with people's souls.[12]

The source of Clark's work is a theological mandate, applying the principles of rhetoric to the deepest theological sense of liberation, reconciliation, and maturation to prevent preachers from tampering with people's souls.

Cannon then offers further definition of the theological and rhetorical partnership by suggesting that, for Clark, a literal, etymological definition of the term *homiletics* is as follows:

> [H]omiletics is composed of the elision of two words, name homily and rhetoric. . . . Clark explains that an elision is where two words are intermixed to form one word and some of the letters in the original words drop out in a new combined word. Thus homiletics is the deliberate syllable-reducing consonantalization of homily and rhetoric.[13]

---

10. Cannon, *Teaching Preaching*, 15.
11. Cannon, *Teaching Preaching*, 13.
12. Cannon, *Teaching Preaching*, 23.
13. Cannon, *Teaching Preaching*, 15.

From the theological side, Cannon states that Clark "illustrates the dynamic hybridity that is fundamental to homiletics" by suggesting that homily, derived from the Greek, "is related to the root word *homoios*, meaning the same, familiar kind."[14] Clark states:

> So the homily of the biblical prophets was made in the name of Jehovah, the same, familiar God of the wandering, nomadic people who the Lord brought up out of slavery, out of the house of bondage. And likewise, the homily of Christians is that God was in Christ reconciling the world, so we, as Christians, can say that Jesus is our homeboy because Jesus is the same, familiar kind of reality to and for us Christians.[15]

Then Clark defines rhetoric, the Greek term that is the second half of the word homiletics:

> Rhetoric is the art of attaching speech to effective logic in persuading, convincing, and edifying the judgment of one's hearers. It means presenting logical evidence using the various techniques of argumentation, in order for preachers to bring to the mind of hearers the "presence" of matters that are of ultimate concern. In other words, rhetoric has to do with understanding how women and men think in order to know what it takes to convince them to buy what we are selling. And whether we know it or not, our task as Professional Proclaimers is to make sales for God concerning Jesus Christ, our homeboy. So, when we add this rhetorical concern to the homily concern, we come up with the term homiletics, which means to express the meaning of the Gospel in a way that women, men, and children can buy it for their living.[16]

Cannon then lays out Clark's homiletical objective by articulating the essence of Black preaching as it has developed from the antebellum era to the present: Black preaching is (1) divine activity, wherein, (2) the word of God is (3) proclaimed or announced (4) on a contemporary issue, (5) with an ultimate response to our God. Cannon says that Clark's

---

14.   Cannon, *Teaching Preaching*, 17.

15.   Cannon, *Teaching Preaching*, 17.

16.   Cannon, *Teaching Preaching*, 18.

five-part definition of preaching is "in the way of all good rhetoric—about the creation of effective oral communication."[17]

For Clark, there are two parts to homiletics, the homily and the rhetoric. The remaining chapters of Canon's book is spent setting forth the sermonic text, offering creative selections and three textual testers, totaling sixteen impressive lectures outlining his homiletical method, approach, and theory. For any preacher or homiletical theorist, Cannon's book is a must read.

While Pipes articulates the value of the liberation partnership of rhetoric and homiletics, and Clark and Cannon define a rhetorical homiletics or what could be called "homily-rhetoric," Andre E. Johnson defines the Black sacred rhetoric of James H. Cone in his early work.

James Cone's Rhetorical Theology Defined

The first time I heard the phrase "rhetorical theology" was in an article by Andre E. Johnson entitled "The Prophetic Persona of James Cone and the Rhetorical Theology of Black Theology."[18] Writing forty years after Cone's seminal work *Black Theology and Black Power*, Johnson argued that Cone not only faced theological challenges in academia, but also rhetorical challenges. To meet both, Cone developed a rhetorical theology. Cone drew upon the rhetoric of Black Power and adopted a prophetic persona "to create not only space and place, but find a voice to articulate his views."[19] Not only did Cone engage a rhetorical theology, but Johnson maintained that if Black theology was to remain a force in academia and the world, it needed to become rhetorical theology.

How then does Johnson define rhetorical theology? Rhetoric, for Johnson, is "discourse, intentionally organized in a message that is goal

---

17. Cannon, *Teaching Preaching*, 18.

18. Andre E. Johnson, "The Prophetic Persona of James Cone and the Rhetorical Theology of Black Theology," *Black Theology: An International Journal* 8, no. 3 (June 2010): 266–85.

19. Johnson, "The Prophetic Persona of James Cone and the Rhetorical Theology of Black Theology," 266.

oriented and seeks to adapt ideas to an audience."[20] Writers and speakers may use the strategy of persona (which we discuss in an upcoming chapter) to "build authority" as well as "invoke cultural traditions of their audience."[21] Rhetorical theology has an unapologetic commitment to the practice of rhetoric based in the following four assumptions.

First, all theology at its core is argument that seeks to persuade and, therefore, is rhetorical. According to Johnson, Christian theology has always been rhetorical because "Christian theology started as a collection of communal arguments, grounded in contextual concerns of everyday life and navigated by a group's collective consensus on texts that spoke volumes on healing the souls of the people."[22]

As I suggested in the introduction, Johnson also argues that all theology needs to make the "rhetorical turn." Johnson quotes David Cunningham in his book, *Faithful Persuasion*:

> Christian theology is best understood as persuasive argument, theologians are involved in debates, disputes and arguments. Theologians are always seeking to persuade others—and to persuade themselves—of a particular understanding of the Christian faith. Therefore, the goal of Christian theology for Cunningham is "faithful persuasion," a theology that speaks in ways faithful to the God of Jesus Christ and persuasive to the world that God has always loved.[23]

Second, rhetorical theology is less focused on theory and more concerned with methods of practice. Cunningham adds in a later work that the discipline and practice of rhetorical theology are concerned with the "practical implications of doctrine."[24] A rhetorical theology does not

---

20. Johnson, "The Prophetic Persona of James Cone and the Rhetorical Theology of Black Theology," 266.

21. Johnson, "The Prophetic Persona of James Cone and the Rhetorical Theology of Black Theology," 268.

22. Johnson, "The Prophetic Persona of James Cone and the Rhetorical Theology of Black Theology," 267.

23. Johnson, "The Prophetic Persona of James Cone and the Rhetorical Theology of Black Theology," 281.

24. Johnson, "The Prophetic Persona of James Cone and the Rhetorical Theology of Black Theology," 281.

"inquire to the truth of a doctrine in a purely abstract sense, instead attention is given to contexts and outcomes."[25] One fundamental context and outcome is attention is given to the ways an audience, within a particular context, is persuaded or moved to act. The rhetorical critic asks: What rhetorical strategies and personas did the speaker use? How did the speaker invite the audience to participate in the theological position that was presented? What does the speaker call the audience to do or be? What is the concrete attitude or action that the discourse crystallizes in the audience?

Third, rhetorical theology is contextual, that is, situated within a particular situation and context, most often defined as the rhetorical situation. Following Lloyd Bitzer, Johnson argues that "the rhetorical situation creates the appropriate and fitting response—or the rhetoric."[26] Rhetoric arises from a "natural context of persons, events, objects, relations, and an exigency which strongly invites utterance."[27] The speaker discerns the times and exegetes the context that (re)creates the rhetorical situation, which leads the speaker to attempt to offer the fitting and appropriate response. Fundamentally, if theology is situated and contextual, it is pulled from the abstract to the practical.

Finally, it is important to note that though rhetorical theology studies the rhetorical situation that gives rise to the response, it only studies how the speaking invited the audience to respond. It does not study how the audience responded, but how the speaker invited the audience to respond—in other words, what the speaker calls the audience to do or be, and the morality of said call.

Johnson argues that Black theology moved away from its roots in James Cone and became more systematic to be more acceptable in the academy, in response to critics who labeled it "pop theology." Ultimately, this meant Black theology was removed from the concerns of the people whom it claimed to represent and began to focus on academic pursuits:

---

25. Johnson, "The Prophetic Persona of James Cone and the Rhetorical Theology of Black Theology," 282.

26. Johnson, "The Prophetic Persona of James Cone and the Rhetorical Theology of Black Theology," 268.

27. Johnson, "The Prophetic Persona of James Cone and the Rhetorical Theology of Black Theology," 268.

Theologians, especially Black theologians, were no longer angry about the situations germane to the masses of Black people. Much, if any, prophetic fire came from scholars who found much to write about in the way they were marginalized in the academy; how tenure was hard to come by, how publications were not plentiful, how religious studies in general still operated from a racist and sexist viewpoint; rather than focusing on more grassroots issues such as how many Black people still suffered on a daily basis.[28]

Johnson concluded by arguing for Black theology to return to its roots as a rhetorical theology, which is an incarnational theology in rhetorical practice.

Donna E. Allen added the rhetorical tool of rhetorical criticism to Black preaching as part of constructing a womanist homiletic. Allen's definition and application of rhetorical criticism opens up a new dimension of the study of African American preaching that I fully embrace and utilize: rhetorical criticism and close reading as a tool to explicate theological meaning and rhetorical symbols in the sermon. An example of rhetorical criticism as a tool are the chapters whereupon I study Lincoln's Second Inaugural and Donald J. Trump's Rose Garden Speech. Let's look at both Allen's work and Kimberly P. Johnson's utilization of rhetorical criticism to analyze and clarify womanist preaching.[29]

Rhetorical Criticism and a Womanist Homiletic

Donna E. Allen presents a critical analysis of Black sacred rhetoric and definitively moves to fully establish a womanist homiletic.[30] Allen believes that a womanist homiletic contributes significantly to the understanding of Black sacred rhetoric by challenging the patriarchy and sexism of the

---

28. Johnson, "The Prophetic Persona of James Cone and the Rhetorical Theology of Black Theology," 283.

29. Donna E. Allen, *Towards a Womanist Homiletic: Katie Cannon, Alice Walker, and Emancipatory Proclamation* (New York: Peter Lang, 2014), and Kimberly P. Johnson, *The Womanist Preacher: Proclaiming Womanist Rhetoric from the Pulpit* (Lanham, MD: Lexington Books, 2017).

30. Allen, *Toward a Womanist Homiletic.*

African American preaching tradition. She utilizes Katie Cannon's work, following Cannon's methodology of Alice Walker's definition of womanism, praxis-oriented womanist critique, rhetorical criticism of black preaching, and Aristotle's rhetorical category of logos to foster an "emancipatory praxis." Allen's goal is to build on the work of Walker and Cannon and offer a womanist paradigm that analyzes the sermons of Black women, one that delimits negative, insulting, and disparaging views of Black women and unmasks "the themes of womanist thought in the performance and content of the preaching of Black women."[31]

Because, for Katie Cannon, womanist preaching is "trans-rational," that is, "an act of embodiment and performed identity," and therefore significantly more than a rational mode of communication. Allen contends that it is necessary for critical analysis of Black sermons to extend beyond Cannon's appropriation of Aristotle's concept of logos (the words, content, and line of reasoning in proclamation) to include the final two means of persuasion, ethos (the very person and presence of the preacher) and pathos (the emotional identifications wrought in preaching).[32] What is even more foundational for Cannon, and therefore Allen, is the use of rhetorical criticism in furthering Cannon's womanist agenda. Allen says:

> In a womanist homiletic, rhetorical criticism is an investigative and constructive paradigm for equipping the preacher and the audience to critically engage the rhetoric of sermons and formulate an emancipatory response.[33]

Cannon's womanist critique of Black sacred rhetoric is a rhetorical criticism of Black preaching that helps the Black community change their sacred rhetoric to eliminate derogatory images of women and patriarchal practices.[34] For Allen, Black preaching is inherently theological and rhetorical, and, to fully engage the preaching of womanists, one must engage rhetorical criticism. At the end of her book, Allen creates a typology of nine emancipatory praxes/themes for womanist preaching of which

---

31. Allen, *Toward a Womanist Homiletic*, 5.

32. Allen, *Toward a Womanist Homiletic*, 6.

33. Allen, *Toward a Womanist Homiletic*, 27.

34. Allen, *Toward a Womanist Homiletic*, 9.

rhetoric is one: the adopting of a rhetorical stance to make effective use of Christian rhetoric.[35]

To understand Allen's definition of rhetorical criticism, we must look closely at her definition of rhetoric, and then sacred rhetoric. Allen defines rhetoric as "actions human beings perform when they use symbols for the purpose of communicating with one another."[36] The scope of rhetoric is extensive and pervades most human cultures and societies, including intuitive or nonverbal symbols, as well as rational verbal symbols. Sacred rhetoric is then "the actions humans perform when they use verbal and non-verbal symbols for the purpose of communication with one another about God."[37]

Following communications and feminist rhetorical theories scholar Sonja K. Foss, Allen defines rhetorical criticism as the ability to understand the various options available to speakers in the construction of messages, and how they work together to create effects in the message. Rhetorical criticism allows the rhetorical critic to see with greater clarity the persuasive choices made by the preacher, and potentially other choices that were not selected. For example, what audience was not mentioned, or who, in effect, was written out of or even excluded from the sermon? For Allen, rhetorical criticism is critical in the construction of a womanist homiletic because it can identify "derogatory images of women and patriarchal teachings" that sometimes consciously or unconsciously are embedded in the sermon. Preachers are making decisive rhetorical choices that include or exclude audiences and affect the audience's comprehension of the message.

Rhetorical criticism is vital because it allows listeners to ascertain, and potentially question, the rhetorical choices made in the construction of sermons because listeners can see rhetorical possibilities other than those selected by the speaker. This ability to perceive other possibilities and question or affirm the speaker's choices is at the heart of rhetorical criticism. A womanist homiletic would make this skill available to congregations to

---

35. Allen, *Toward a Womanist Homiletic*, 82.

36. Allen, *Toward a Womanist Homiletic*, 8.

37. Allen, *Toward a Womanist Homiletic*, 8.

help congregation and preacher move to an "emancipatory praxis." Listeners would be equipped with a model that allows them to critically engage the sermon. In emancipatory praxis, "preaching a sermon is, by definition, a mutual rhetorical act."[38] Preaching is an art predicated on a set of developed and honed skills by both preacher and listener. In the Black preaching tradition, the sermon is a dialogue, a communal art form, "where all the artists (preacher and congregation) can fine tune their skills."[39] In that communal reflection, the rhetoric of the sermon can be examined and emancipatory praxis is determined regarding a faithful response to the preached word. Allen, following Cannon, says that "listeners from pulpit and pew, together, shape the faith praxis and sacred rhetoric of the community."[40]

Allen then applies the concept of a womanist homiletic to the womanist preaching of Prathia Laura Ann Hall. Allen suggests that a womanist homiletic "is helpful for understanding the art of preaching by womanist preachers because it enables one to appreciate what a womanist is doing in sermonizing."[41] Hall's womanist preaching challenges racism, classism, sexism, heterosexism, and homophobia. She preached a womanist and gender inclusive gospel in a time when her words were not welcomed by many. By her insightful analysis of Hall, Allen clarifies in exacting detail how a womanist homiletic both challenges and expands the Black preaching tradition.

The addition of rhetorical criticism to African American preaching again reinforces my argument that African American preaching is inherently theological and rhetorical. In every sermon, the preacher communicates a belief system, not only verbally, but also nonverbally with gestures, sound, and so forth. When we look through the lens of rhetorical criticism at the belief system (theology), we can notice how the belief system of a specific preacher, in a specific cultural context, forms the audience and

---

38. Allen, *Toward a Womanist Homiletic*, 12.

39. Allen, *Toward a Womanist Homiletic*, 12.

40. Allen, *Toward a Womanist Homiletic*, 12.

41. Allen, *Toward a Womanist Homiletic*, 6.

predisposes the audience to act (rhetoric). Preaching is inherently theological and rhetorical.

Allen's work is a major contribution to the Black preaching tradition, challenging the rhetorical dominance of the African American heterosexual male by clarifying the emancipatory praxis of womanist preaching and opening up new windows of analysis of Black preaching, such as the inclusion of rhetorical criticism as part of homiletical inquiry.

Womanist Rhetoric and Womanist Preaching

Kimberly P. Johnson, in *The Womanist Preacher*, makes explicit the connection between womanist theology and Black preaching in order to articulate a theory and method of womanist preaching.[42] While many African American male preachers wax eloquent about liberation and social justice, in reality, as Johnson quotes James Cone, "it is amazing that many black male ministers, young and old, can hear the message of liberation in the gospel when related to racism but remain deaf to a similar message in the context of sexism."[43] Because womanism has undoubtedly been underarticulated within academic disciplines, Johnson's purpose is "to bring awareness to the historical art form that exists in womanist preaching and womanist rhetoric."[44] With the exception of Donna E. Allen, Elaine Flake, Katie Cannon, Marsha Houston, and Olga Idriss Davis, most womanist scholarship focuses on theory, theology, hermeneutics, methodology, or praxis, but not discourse and communication.[45] As a communication scholar and ordained minister of the gospel, Johnson's focus is to articulate

---

42. Johnson, *The Womanist Preacher*.

43. Johnson, *The Womanist Preacher*, 2.

44. Johnson, *The Womanist Preacher*, xxii.

45. See Allen, *Towards a Womanist Homiletic*; Elaine Flake, *God in Her Midst: Preaching Healing to Wounded Women* (Valley Forge: Judson Press, 2007); Katie Geneva Cannon, "Womanist Interpretation and Preaching in the Black Church," in *Searching the Scriptures*, Volume I: *A Feminist Introduction I*, ed. Elisabeth Schussler Fiorenza (New York: Crossroads, 1994); and "Theorizing African American Women's Discourse," in *Centering Ourselves: African American Feminist and Womanist Studies of Discourse*, ed. Marsha Houston and Olga Idriss Davis (New York: Hampton, 2002).

a rhetorical theology of the womanist discourse of African American preaching. What is unique and a major contribution to African American preaching and womanist thought is her exploration of how womanist preaching attempts to transform/adapt the theological tenets of womanist thought to make it rhetorically viable in the preaching ministry of the church, another form of emancipatory praxis.

Johnson demonstrates the rhetorical viability of womanist preaching by exploring the sermons of five preachers in the Black church who are considered exemplars of womanist preaching: Elaine Flake, Gina Stewart, Cheryl Kirk-Duggan, Melva L. Sampson, and Claudette Copeland. She analyzes their sermons based on the four different tenets Stacey Floyd-Thomas utilizes to represent Walker's four tenets of womanist thought, which I define briefly:

> *Radical subjectivity*—ways women have been able to subvert forced hegemonic identities of a racist-sexist world; the "radicality" of self and Black women speaking truth to power in the face of formidable odds.
>
> *Traditional communalism*—ways cultural traditions have nurtured and supported Black women on individual and collective journeys toward liberation, while at the same time calling Black women back to their foundational values.
>
> *Redemptive self-love*—unashamed self-love and standing up for self.
>
> *Critical engagement*—critical evaluation of society's cultural norms.

Johnson applies Floyd-Thomas's theological conceptual framework to the art of Black preaching to help readers homiletically "comprehend what womanist revolutionary acts of rebellion look like."[46] In the vein of Donna E. Allen and following rhetorical critical scholar Michael Charles Leff, Johnson uses close reading as a form of rhetorical criticism to uncover what preachers are actually doing in order to determine whether or not the sermons really do transform/adapt womanist thought. She also

---

46. Johnson, *The Womanist Preacher*, xxiii.

develops four rhetorical models of womanist preaching that diagram the various rhetorical strategies, sermonic functions, and methodological approaches used by Flake, Stewart, Kirk-Duggan, Sampson, and Copeland.

Rhetorical criticism allows the critic to see who was included, the theology that forms the basis of the inclusion or, in this case, the four tenets of Stacey Floyd-Thomas. Rhetoric and the art of rhetorical criticism allow the critic to see the theology and how it works in calling audiences to respond with particular acts—in this case, to liberate African American women from their physical, mental, and emotional abuse by reimagining a woman from being a victim of circumstance to being victorious over her current situation with radical subjectivity, traditional communalism, redemptive self-love, and critical engagement.

As a final summary of Johnson's work, I share a definition of womanist preaching she sent in response to my email query: "Womanist preaching is a homiletical methodology that challenges the patriarchal and oppressive forces that enslave women and rob them of their self-esteem. This method of preaching seeks to liberate, affirm, and empower women by centering the lived experiences of women, by culturally critiquing and countering conventional interpretations of the Bible as well as society at large, and by giving voice to those who are silenced."

WHY HAVE SOME SO MUCH AND OTHERS SO LITTLE?

What the poor need is not charity but capital, not caseworkers but coworkers. And what the rich need is a wise, honorable and just way of divesting themselves of their overabundance.

—Clarence Jordan

Every person has a constellation of culture, family of origin, and, for many, ecclesiastical systems that influence, raise, and develop us from the earliest stages of life. Such systems include categories of gender, ethnicity, social and economic location and class, as well as conditions of physical and mental health. Out of this constellation, most people ask existential questions about the meaning of life and living. For example, in his book *Decoded*, business mogul and rapper Jay-Z says this:

> I was always fascinated by religion and curious about people's different ideas. And like everyone, I've always wanted answers to the basic questions. Still, by the time I reached my teens, the only time I'd be anywhere near a church was when someone I knew died, and even then, I wouldn't necessarily go in. But I wasn't looking for church anyway; I was looking for an explanation.[1]

---

1. Jay-Z, *Decoded* (New York: Spiegel and Grau, 2011), 276.

I interpret this comment to mean that the church was not dealing in any significant way, from Jay-Z's perspective, with the basic questions of life he was asking. He does not explicitly state what his questions were. But I wonder if one might have been why, when he experienced Fifth Avenue in Times Square and other affluent areas in New York and New York State, he saw ostentatious luxury, overflowing abundance, and outrageous wealth, but when he came home to Marcy Projects in Brooklyn, he saw abject poverty, persistent violence, lack of economic resources, crime, and human brokenness in nearly every direction. If his question in some form was why do some have so much and his community have so little, and the church, especially in his community, does not respond to that question, we might be wise to conclude that, for him, the church was not relevant. This would result in only going to church for a funeral, and then possibly not going in. The theology that the church was espousing did not answer his questions.

Like my interpretation of Jay-Z's question, the distribution of resources is one of my essential questions in life: why do some have so much and some have so little. I am not uncritically "hating on" people who have. I believe wealth is much more nuanced than the easy, opposite, antagonistic, and often extreme poles of discourse around individual merit on one hand and social theft on the other. I subscribe to what Thomas Piketty says:

> Every fortune is partially justified yet potentially excessive. Outright theft is rare, as is absolute merit. . . . Broadly speaking, the return on capital often inextricably combines elements of true entrepreneurial labor (an absolutely indispensable force for economic development), pure luck (one happens at the right moment to buy a promising asset at a good price), and outright theft. The arbitrariness of wealth accumulation is a much broader phenomenon than the arbitrariness of inheritance.[2]

In a nuanced and mixed morality, it is possible to view America from this lens: (1) encounter pure luck that a continent is so rich with resources, (2) by deceit and murder heist the land from indigenous peoples,

---

2. Thomas Piketty, *Capital in the Twenty-First Century*, trans. Arthur Goldhammer (London: Belknap Press of Harvard University, 2014), 444–46.

(3) secure free labor for hundreds of years via the inhumane and racial crime of chattel slavery, Jim Crow, and such, (4) exploit and crush laborers and immigrants in the period of industrialization, and (5) apply entrepreneurial ingenuity and inventiveness to pure luck, theft of land, ownership of another person's body, cheap labor, and gain massive and unimaginable wealth.

I am also aware that once one gains wealth, one has the ability to unduly influence government policy to create even more wealth for oneself, ensuring the uneven division of resources, including the structuring of moderate wealth winners (the middle class) and deserving losers (the poor). As a prime and very simple example of picking winners and losers, one only need think of GI soldiers who came from WWII and the resources available to white GIs to build wealth, which were not available to African American GIs by decree and force of law. Or, what the law was not structured to accomplish, mob violence made sure of: Black people were losers. An example is the Tulsa Race Riots of 1921, a massacre by white residents of three hundred Black residents, leaving ten thousand Black people homeless and destroying the town's and nation's most thriving Black business district. Capital, in reality, is a social and political construct that creates inordinate wealth disparity and principally benefits an oligarchical few. Of prime interest is this: what is the theological justification as to why some get health care and others do not, some get access to decent housing and some do not. In other words, who has wealth, resources, legitimacy, freedom, access, and power, and who does not? My rhetorical theology leads me to a universal and dangerous God wanting benefit for all, rather than a particular and cultural tribal god who justifies the mixed morality of the haves and dismisses the have-nots as immoral losers.

I believe the poverty of the have-nots is as nuanced as the wealth of the haves. All poverty is partially justified by social environment, yet affected by individual life decisions and choices within that social environment. Poverty is much more nuanced than the easy, opposite, antagonistic, and extreme poles of discourse of moral failures and outright laziness on one hand and the bright light of merit as the universal ticket to escape poverty on the other. Broadly speaking, poverty is the inability to benefit from the capital of one's own labor, bad luck to be born in communities where few moments are presented to buy a promising asset at a good price, and outright discrimination in the form of institutional racism and oppression to limit and discourage equal opportunity at every hand.

My rhetorical theology has many conversation partners, several that I will discuss in this chapter—such as theological ethics, public theology, anthropology, and Christian realism—all in the attempt to discern how resources are divided up and justified in the name of God. I simply want to know why some have so much and others have so little, and what does God and theology have to do with it?

Public theology has a strong commonality with rhetorical theology.

Rhetorical Theology and Public Theology

Largely in the context of complicit and acquiescent assent by the majority white culture, for generations African American men and women have also dealt with the issue of police violence, such as slave patrols, legal enforcement of racist Black Codes, Jim Crow laws, concepts of "law and order," the "War on Drugs," mass incarceration, and racial profiling. Throughout this history, there have been seminal events that serve as cause and container for massive expressions of public protest. On May 25, 2020, the death of George Floyd at the hands of Minneapolis police galvanized an intergenerational mass movement by many Americans to demand just and fair policing and eradication of aspects of systemic and institutional racism. Several other contemporary flash points had already been boiling—the deaths of Trayvon Martin, Tamir Rice, Sandra Bland, and Breonna Taylor, to mention but a few of many. For the purpose of defining public theology, August 9, 2014, the date of the death of Michael Brown at the hands of police in Ferguson, Missouri, is instructive.[3]

3.　See Leah Gunning Francis, *Faith and Ferguson: Sparking Leadership and Awakening Community* (St. Louis: Chalice, 2015).

Katie Day and Sebastian Kim in the introduction to their edited volume *A Companion to Public Theology* point out that six months after the police killing of Brown, many faith-based leaders from around the country returned to Ferguson for a public rally of clergy, religious leaders, and community members. Michael-Ray Matthews, leader of the PICO Network (People Involved in Community Organizing), a coalition of religious groups, wrote:

> As I continued to lead songs and chants in the pouring rain, one of the seminarians grabbed the bullhorn and asked if we could change our chant from "show me what democracy looks like" to "show me what theology looks like." She was calling her sisters and brothers in the faith to go *all in*—to be totally immersed in mind, body and spirit, to bring the richness of our faith into the public space.[4]

Public theology shows what theology looks like by engagement of Christian theology and ethics with social issues to build the common good for a fair and just society for all, and for some to foster, in Christian terms, the very "reign of God." It is important to note that persons on the "right" and "left" do public theology differently. White evangelicals interpret America as a "Christian" nation, promote a resulting Christian nationalism that we discuss in the next section, and engage social and political action around such issues as religious liberty, abortion, conservative judges, and the like. On the other hand, many minority communities interpret theology and social and political action around racial justice, equality for LGBTQI rights, women's rights, economic justice, human trafficking, climate change, and similar causes.

David Tracy asked the critical question as to what the "public" in public theology meant and identified three publics that public theology seeks to engage in meaningful dialogue: society (political sectors), the academy (academia), and the church (religious). He suggests that, given these publics, speaking only in church language exclusively understood by those of the church forms a "privileged rationality." In public theology, the

---

4. Sebastian Kim and Katie Day, *A Companion to Public Theology*, Brill's Companions to Modern Theology, vol. 1 (Boston: Leiden, 2017), 1–24.

language should be openly accessible by all and not couched in theologically elitist and esoteric terms.

After Tracy, E. Harold Breitenberg, Jr., in his article, "To Tell the
Truth: Will the Real Public Theology Please Stand Up?" distinguished
public theology from civil or public religion, political theology, public
church, public philosophy, and public or social ethics. After reviewing the
proliferating literature under the rubric of public theology, he concludes
that there is enough consensus to be able to define public theology as:

> theologically informed public discourse about public issues, addressed to
> the church, synagogue, mosque, temple or other religious bodies, as well
> as the larger public or publics, argued in ways that can be evaluated and
> judged by publicly available warrants and criteria.[5]

In the last line, "judged by publicly available warrants and criteria" means
that the church cannot escape into uncritical and unquestionable God
claims through appeals to revelation alone. All God claims and revelation
are subject to publicly available warrants and rational discourse.

Day and Kim note that careful observation presents several common
traits or markers of public theology that shares mutuality with rhetorical
theology. First, public theology is often incarnational, meaning seeking to
be relevant to people both inside and outside of the church. For Day and
Kim, public theology is deeply indebted to Dietrich Bonhoeffer (1906–
1945) as "a continuing source of theological grounding." They recite a
recurring theme of Bonhoeffer, concreteness.[6]

Public incarnational theology is concrete and challenges the insularity
and exclusivity of theology in academia. Theology that is only addressed
to the church and understandable only in the academy is divorced from
lived life and ceases, in its essence, to be relevant. For some, the church is
in fact apart from the world and transcendent of many day-to-day social
concerns and issues. Others see theology as politically neutral and above
the fracas of human skirmishes; they refuse to endorse or get involved
in concrete public theology, especially from the pulpit. Public theology

---

5. Kim and Day, *A Companion to Public Theology*, 4.

6. Kim and Day, *A Companion to Public Theology*, 10.

focuses on bringing the *evangelion*, or good news of God's intention for all of God's creation, to have the full aspects of human life and social experience rather than be limited by social constructions of race, gender, religion, and class.

Second, Kim and Day expand publics beyond the church, academy, or society of Tracy's initial definition. Kim and Day suggest:

> Theologian Max Stackhouse added a fourth public to the academic, religious and political sectors, which is the economic. Robert Benne appropriated law as another public theology should engage. South African theologian Dirkie Smit identifies four publics with a slightly different emphasis: political, economic, civil society and public opinion.[7]

Across time, scholars suggest more and more publics with which public theology should engage.

Third, public theology is interdisciplinary because it draws on other fields of study in order to be more relevant to society. The critical analysis offered by many fields and disciplines helps to illumine the plight of and suggest powerful remedies for lack of justice and fairness. Public theology must draw on the resources of social sciences including anthropology, economics, geography, history, political science, psychology, rhetoric, social studies, and sociology for dialogue and credibility. Public theology also engages the physical sciences. For example, in order for a public theologian to engage climate justice with credibility, there has to be some acceptance and appreciation of the science behind it.

Day and Kim even suggest: "Some public theologians further advocate the incorporation of informants outside of academic bibliographies. In engaging issues such as poverty or human trafficking, for example, the deepest insights will come from those most directly affected."[8] Public theology is no longer to be found solely in the academy, but in the broad swath of humanity that seeks the common good and offers transcendence and inspiration in the arts.

---

7. Kim and Day, *A Companion to Public Theology*, 12.

8. Kim and Day, *A Companion to Public Theology*, 13.

The fourth mark of public theology is that it is dialogical, with the essential parts of true dialogue including self-critique, transparency, accountability, and honesty about the construction of authority. I once wrote an unpublished reflection, "Can Prophets Be Critiqued?" to express my view that "prophets" in righteous indignation deliver truth to power and, if not careful, cast themselves beyond critique and accountability based in a construction of unquestionable divine authority. Jesus is harsh on those who find faults in others but have a different and less stringent standard of critique for themselves: he calls them hypocrites (Matthew 23:13). This hypocrisy was vividly seen in white evangelicals' enthusiastic and total support of the candidacy, presidency, and post presidency of Donald J. Trump. They spent years decrying same-sex persons and others as immoral under the rubric of the "Moral Majority" or "family values," and yet they did not apply morality and family values to the question of gaining access and influence with power. The white evangelical community lost its moral authority because it refused to be dialogical in the manner of self-critique and accountability.

Day and Kim cite an example of lack of public self-critique and accountability in the epidemic of sexual abuse by clergy. While not exclusively limited to the Roman Catholic Church, the Catholic hierarchy, in no uncertain terms, advocated "traditional marriage" and decried same-gender relationships as a sin, yet at the same time covered up the presence of gay clergy, pedophiles, and the sexual abuse of children.[9] Proclaiming rigid separation of church and state, Catholic leaders were not accountable to the state and advocated they could deal with the issues internally. Others argued that state interference would hinder the free exercise of religion. As a result, particularly early in the long-running scandal, the Catholic Church resisted legal action and media attention when accusations of sexual abuse began to escalate in the last several decades.

Marci Hamilton argues that when making the assumption that religion can only be a social good and, in my words, inherently good, one runs the risk of sacrificing transparency and accountability.[10] Hamilton

9. Kim and Day, *A Companion to Public Theology*, 14.

10. See Marci Hamilton, *God vs. the Gavel: Religion and the Rule of Law* (New York: Cambridge University Press, 2005).

is correct when she asserts that the welfare of citizens is the fundamental responsibility of the state and supersedes the right to the free exercise of religion. In other words, when the health and safety of citizens who do not have full agency (in this case, children) is jeopardized, the state has jurisdiction over religious institutions.

The last part of being dialogical, and maybe the most essential for public theology, is to ask "by what authority?" For some, the authority of theology comes from transcendent sources and revelation. When revelation is based in the transcendent, how can it be challenged? From my perspective, authority is a social construction, mediated through rhetorical processes. Revelation can be challenged by the concrete behavior it induces in its adherents. I challenge divine authority when one's behavior is based in hate, violence, discrimination, abuse, racism, oppression, and the like. I have issues when you tell me that your God told you to come to my country, take my land, and murder my people. Every instance of this kind of religious authority is adherence to a tribal god.

It is easy to make theological pronouncements from a perch above public scrutiny with the cover of God, revelation, and theology, but if those pronouncements do not line up with moral practice based in transparency, accountability, honesty, and self-critique, the public is excluded from theological formulation. The church is viewed as insular, irreverent, and irrelevant, and can easily and often slip into the path of violence rather than peace and healing.

According to Kim and Day, the fifth mark of public theology is its global perspective. Kim and Day recount that globalization is a well-documented phenomenon often expressed as the knitting together of cultures, economies, technologies, politics, and religions into an increasingly interactive reality often experienced and described as a shrinking of the world. For our purposes, realizing and slightly diverging away from the most common and generalized understanding of globalization, I am interested in the globalizing of theologies of liberation. We must more readily identify, learn from, and engage global theologies of struggle and resistance such as the Confessing Church in Germany in the 1930s; anti-apartheid theology expressed most clearly and definitively in the 1985

61

and 1986 revised version of the Kairos document; liberation theology of the Latin American context; Black, feminist, womanist, and queer theology of the United States; Black theology of South Africa; Palestinian liberation theology; Dalit theology in India; and Minjung theology in South Korea. There are many more liberative theologies that could be included, but suffice it to say all public theologies could be strengthened by drawing and learning from each other as well as understanding global trends of oppression, the upcoming global racial hierarchy we will discuss.

The final distinguishing mark of public theology, and maybe the most difficult of all for scholars, is that public theology is not only to be examined and written about in publications, but it is *performed* in public spaces. Public theology is performed with one's physical presence ,with Martin Luther King Jr. as an example that I cite in *How to Preach a Dangerous Sermon*:

> In regard to equality envisioned and represented by physical presence, the most obvious fact is that the "I've Been to the Mountaintop" speech/sermon was only possible because King brought his concern and physical presence to Memphis to help sanitation workers. This was an act of solidarity in a long list of acts of solidarity for movements of freedom and equality starting in 1954 with the Montgomery bus boycott. King put his concern and physical presence on the line in numerous ways every day of the civil rights movement as he was jailed; stabbed; assaulted with rocks and bricks; battered psychologically with jeers, hate-filled names and messages, death threats, pressure, harassment, and manipulations; this even from his own government. King was ultimately shot and killed because of his work for peace and justice, because of his concern for the vulnerable, and in this instance, the sanitation workers in Memphis.[11]

This physical presence challenges the boundary between action and reflection. As evidenced in the public response to the killing of George Floyd by #BlackLivesMatter and others, action challenges and informs theology, and theology enlightens activism. Public theology is performed, and not just published in books and articles.

---

11. Frank Thomas, *How to Preach a Dangerous Sermon* (Nashville: Abingdon Press, 2018), 45.

Before leaving public theology, I must mention one of the most common critiques of public theology: the inherent difficulty and tension of being publicly relevant and yet retaining Christian distinctiveness. Public theology can be so Christian as to be irrelevant to the public or, on the other hand, be so relevant to the church alone that it bears no Christian witness.

The Global Racial Paradigm

In the introduction to this book, my brief overview of Reinhold Niebuhr posits an analysis of America's racial moral hierarchy that, as Cornel West says, "reveals and challenges the persistence of power, greed, and conflict beneath the surface of order." I want to return to that discussion in regards to Christian realism as an aspect of rhetorical theology. It is important first to treat in more detail the work of Roger Sanjek, whose primary argument is that race and racism is a post-1400s invention to justify European global conquest and expansion.

Roger Sanjek and the Enduring Inequalities of Race

The globalized racial hierarchy orders perceptions, shapes social and political policy, orders and makes possible wealth for some and not so much for others, influences religion, and dictates a pervasive global racism. Again, based in the 1400s European period of expansion, Africa, the "New World," Asia, and the Pacific were "encountered, renamed, mapped, economically penetrated, reordered, politically dominated, and assigned" places in what Michel-Rolph Trouillot calls "the international hierarchy of races, colors, religions, and cultures."[12] Gilbert Murray, a turn-of-the-twentieth-century British imperialist, captures the essence of this racialized global view (italics are mine):

---

12. Steven Gregory and Roger Sanjek, eds., *Race* (New Brunswick, NJ: Rutgers University Press, 1996), 1.

There is in the world a hierarchy of races . . . those nations which eat more, claim more and get higher wages, will direct and rule the others, and the *lower work of the world* will tend in the long run to be done *by lower breeds of man*. This much *we of the ruling color* will no doubt accept as obvious.[13]

This statement is indicative of a racialized worldview expressing itself in a suffocating moral hierarchy. Earlier, in *How to Preach a Dangerous Sermon* and *Surviving a Dangerous Sermon*, I spoke principally of the American context and named it "moral hierarchy." Sanjek helps us to identity and locate it as an international hierarchy of races, colors, religions, and cultures.

For Sanjek, there is a difference between the historical and ever-present ethnocentric attitudes toward neighboring societies (we are better than them) or the more tolerant live-and-let-live mindset (their customs are different), and racist moral hierarchy. The vast difference is that culture and skin color were tightly linked in thirteenth-century racial ideology. Inferior status was/is a result of inherited racial constitution and features based in the unquestioned consequence of birth. As an example, what made American chattel slavery more devastating than earlier versions of slavery was the utilization of racial identity as the basis and justification for enslavement.

This racial moral hierarchy has done devastating harm to people all over the globe related to human worth, dignity, and personhood. It has "transformed and deformed the life courses and psyches of its victims, and also of its beneficiaries."[14] Its reality is not based in anything other than "the conquest, dispossession, enforced transportation, and economic exploitation of human beings over five centuries."[15] The legacy of these systems is that millions of people still today have accepted these invented racial categories as "fixed in nature and believe and interpret the systemic qualities of racist social orders as based on 'real' differences among 'real' races."[16] These racist categories and their social order are still expediting

13. Gregory and Sanjek, eds., *Race*, 1.

14. Gregory and Sanjek, eds., *Race*, 1–2.

15. Gregory and Sanjek, eds., *Race*, 1–2.

16. Gregory and Sanjek, eds., *Race*, 1–2.

and justifying global oppression on this very day and in this very moment, as I take this very breath.

In the 1970s, according to Sanjek, as a result of the attempt to mask this racial hierarchy, "ethnicity" came to center stage in anthropological studies and American life. The effect was the attempt to erase racism or push it aside altogether for many Americans. The research and much that followed in the 1970s stressed that African Americans needed to be understood and to accept their status as an ethnic group working their way up the ladder as had European and other immigrants. Historic inequality as a result of systemic racism was downplayed, and "good" racial relations were styled as ethnic relations based upon the perception that African Americans had the same opportunity as other "ethnic" groups in America.

This view also portrayed white ethnic groups as maintaining their "ethnicity," that is, old world cultural values for generations after their arrival as immigrants. Sanjek argues that this 1970s neoconservative insistence on white ethnic group persistence was suspect and a hoax and that, in fact, the masses of European immigrants during the nineteenth and twentieth centuries adopted American white racial status, what he calls "Angloconformity," and paid the price of cultural loss and linguistic extinction (italics are mine):

> The outcome of Angloconformity for non-British European immigrants has been an opportunity to share "race" with whites with whom they do not share "class." . . . It also explains in part the unease and the antagonism with which many white Americans view linguistic and cultural survival and resurgence among Americans of color, those for whom the Angloconformist road to white racial status has not been an option. Some degree of *envy or turmoil perhaps accompanies the prize of race awarded upon the surrender of ethnicity.*[17]

Angloconformity, that is, American white racial status, was not an option for most persons of color and therefore the attempt to erase the aggressive cultural identity of persons of color and the postulation of comfortable and contorted "color blindness" is an attempt to cloak the global racialized order and replace the protestations of people of color with the

---

17. Gregory and Sanjek, eds., *Race*, 9.

envy and turmoil of white grievance. Even for many adopters of white racialized status who are not directly benefiting from unregulated capitalism, the unspoken words are: "Despite my class, I am still white." Domination is what the globalized racial hierarchy teaches, what many whites have been taught all their lives. When, as we said earlier, the domination myth falls apart, then they lose meaning for their lives.[18] For Angloconformity to admit the existence of globalized racial hierarchy (systemic racism), based upon unfettered capitalism at the core of American life, is for whites to give up critical aspects of identity and privileged racial status.

Globalized racial hierarchy has provided a convenient myth of American individualism, America as the "new" promised land, poverty as a moral state of being, and the indulgence, in my terms, of a "winner theology," meaning that the privileged classes believe that they "won" because they were the most moral, despite the level of immorality and theft that it took to win. Winner theology of white racial status blames blacks, women, immigrants, the LGBTQI community, and the poor rather than rejecting racial hierarchy and adopting the struggle of racial equality.

I have been talking exclusively in the language of black and white. The post-1400s global racial order is extended well beyond the ranking of races as singularly black and white, but Sanjek utilizes these two stark terms to define the poles of racial hierarchy. Therefore, given the reality of the suffocating post-1400s moral hierarchy of races, colors, and religions, I want to return to Reinhold Niebuhr's Christian realism to help us to see the global racialized hierarchy at work and help us articulate more succinctly the bifurcated nature of individual and group morals and theology that justifies global racialized hierarchy.

The Christian Realism of Reinhold Niebuhr

In the justice work of Martin Luther King Jr., James Cone, and many others, the Christian realism of Reinhold Niebuhr has been important to critical reflection and decisive action. Niebuhr was absolutely correct when he postulated that human beings are normally driven by self-interest

18. Thomas, *How to Preach a Dangerous Sermon*, "Shrinking Whiteness in America," 10–13.

and, as a result of the quest to compound and heighten that self-interest, are inherently anxious. Because life itself is fragile, based in the reality of the impermanence of all things and the ever-present fear and belief that mortal enemies are immediate and over the next proverbial hill, anxious human beings seek to insulate, fortify, and protect themselves. In fact, the anxiety is so high for many that they exaggerate real and perceived threats, making them so large and ominous that these people become perpetually disturbed and troubled. The only resolution is to make themselves the center of the world. In the attempt to calm our anxiety, we practice idolatry and replace God with ourselves. This prideful idolatry leads to global racial hierarchy, resulting in some of the most vicious, violent, cruel, destructive, and evil behavior towards others, particularly against those not members of our group, and most of it with religious justifications in the name of God.

While we are very anxious about safety and power, we are also artistic, intellectual, moral, and religious beings. Inherently, Niebuhr believed that we seek after truth and know that our truth is only partial. Our fretful and prideful idolatry is coupled with even more anxiety over the relativity of our truth, and so we claim our truth to be ultimate and absolute. We assert true and absolute moral judgments, and then construct a God that absolutely blesses and condones our absolutism. Our moral judgments are righteous and just and our opponents are completely wrong and evil. In the words of Niebuhr, "the most serious sin of all is that we claim our spirits to represent the divine, and our religion to be God's religion."[19] Niebuhr's comment is similar to that of Karl Marx:

> The beginning of all criticism is the criticism of religion. For it is on this ultimate level that the pretensions of men reach their most absurd form. The final sin is always committed in the name of religion.[20]

In the arena of religion, human pretensions reach their most absurd practice in the form of absolutism.

19. Langdon Gilkey, introduction to Niebuhr's *Moral Man and Immoral Society*, xxii.

20. Martin E. Marty, "Public Theology and the American Experience," *The Journal of Religion* 54, no. 4 (October 1974): 332–59.

Niebuhr postulated that only the highly unusual individual could in their spiritual pride claim to be the center of the universe by themselves. Most assert this claim together through the community of which they are a part: family, tribe, religion, nation, gender, profession, or church. The number of people who have thought through their moral values deeply, profoundly, and carefully, and therefore are able to discriminate between good and evil, is very small. Without this necessary level of careful and critical moral analysis, it is easier to place the interest of the group as central to one's thought, belief, and action. Human beings give loyalty, power, and legitimacy to the group and often uncritically operate out of "group think." Regardless of the facts, many people blindly follow the opinion of the leader(s) of the group. Our trusted leader(s) establish truth—what is right and wrong, and who is friend and enemy. Good is what my leader and group does and evil is what the other side does, regardless of the moral merits of behavior. We are committed to establish group security and success by conquest and domination of competing groups. Thus, the pride and group think of communities becomes the religion and allows the community to make an idol of itself, and each community member bows down and worships, often without any critical reflection on systems and orders such as globalized racial hierarchy.

No community can make this admission that they are the center of the world because the idolatry is too devastating to admit. Human beings deceive themselves by rationalizing that what they do is right, boldly labeling it as their spiritual and moral obligation. Throughout human history, nations and people go to war mainly for self-interest and execute other dastardly deeds such as lynching, which we will discuss later in the chapter, and yet cloak their self-interest and violence in the pretension of defending God, sacred tradition, or peace, order, democracy, and their "way of life." It is very difficult for either individuals or communities to admit their brazen self-interest. The hypocrisy can easily be seen by those outside the group, because as soon as their professed "values" run against their self-interest, the group abandons stated values, such as "liberty and justice for all" or "democracy," in shameless ploys of raw and naked power. In reality, these values are only for the benefit of their group. It is the height of moral difficulty for communities or individuals to admit to self-interest even as their practice is contradictory to the very values proclaimed, such as in Christian support and executions of lynching in America.

Niebuhr found that American citizens characteristically behaved idolatrously, and churches provided little critique of this tendency. Niebuhr thought that the god of American religions (the so-called American dream) was an American god, or what I would call a tribal god. Niebuhr used the business community and the uncritical devotion to the "free enterprise system" as direct evidence of national idolatry as the "American way of life." As evidence of idolatry, Niebuhr argued there is not one church in a thousand where the moral problems of industrial civilization (free enterprise) are discussed with sufficient realism from the pulpit. Most homilies and sermons are irrelevant in the realm of "human actions or attitudes in any problem of collective behavior."[21] From his perspective, "chumminess" invalidates the universal appeal of the gospel. Having been a pastor, Niebuhr concludes that prophets almost have to be itinerants:

> Critics of the church think we preachers are afraid to tell the truth because we are economically dependent upon the people of the church. There is something in that, but it does not quite get to the root of the matter. . . . I think the real clue to the tameness of preacher is the difficulty one finds in telling unpleasant truths to people whom one has learned to love.[22]

While idolatry and hypocrisy are the major forms of sin in history, most American religion emphasizes personal sin and individual immoralities. Focus on personal and individual sin allows people to be individually "good" and "moral," and yet boldly sin through the pride and cruelty of their group. People will support immoral actions of their group and justify to themselves that they are moral because of their behavior on the individual level. This explains the sharp moral distinction between the individual who purports to be governed by ethics and the group that must

---

21.   Marty, "Public Theology and the American Experience," 335.

22.   Marty, "Public Theology and the American Experience," 344.

rely upon the "political policies which a purely individualistic ethic must always find embarrassing."[23]

As a result of political practices void of ethics, power destroys peace between communities because, for Niebuhr, conflict and coercion are always necessary to secure peace. Individuals are, in some cases, able to overcome egotism and through empathy consider the interest of others. Groups, on the other hand, are incapable of such behavior. The collective egoism or idolatry of the group expresses itself at a higher, bolder, and more brazen level, causing intergroup conflict where the only alternative is coercion to secure peace. Niebuhr believed that coercion and conflict remain the same regardless of who is in power, because if one group gains power and coerces the other, when the other gets power, it will return the favor. This insures injustice and competitive rivalry among groups.

In light of this cycle of inevitable coercion and injustice, human beings must reject the notion of an ideal society. The idealistic quest for an uncoerced and perfect peace must be jettisoned for the realistic goal of proximate justice. As Niebuhr says: "there will be enough justice, and . . . coercion will be sufficiently nonviolent to prevent this common enterprise from issuing into complete disaster."[24] Niebuhr rejected the idealism that individuals and groups could achieve the heights of agape love revealed in the life and death of Jesus. Without question, love is the absolute ethical standard, but the sin of self-interest is so entrenched that love could never be achieved, and the best that could be accomplished is justice, a balance of power among competing groups. Justice rather than love was placed at the center of Christian ethics.

Niebuhr did not believe that increasing rational intelligence or religious fervor based in a revival of religion could deliver human beings from the sin of self-interest and the resulting social chaos. When self-interest is involved, rationality often gives sway to irrational forces or the group's interest, and religion seems to guide individual behavior but fails when applied to collective political life, when it blesses group self-interest.

---

23. Niebuhr, *Moral Man and Immoral Society*, xxix.

24. Niebuhr, *Moral Man and Immoral Society*, 22.

In light of this reality of absolutism, true religion—genuine personal salvation—is facing the divine transcendence and admitting the partiality and the falsity of one's spiritual pride. Without the initial repentance of anxiety, pride, and idolatry based in an encounter with divine judgment, religion, cloaked in the absolute, becomes self-interest and idolatry, service to a tribal God. If human power in history is based upon self-interest, then the revelation of divine goodness must counter that power with what the world believes is weakness. As a result, the Christ is led as a lamb to the slaughter. God's revelation "transvalues" human values and turns them upside down by death on a cross.

James Cone Critiques Reinhold Niebuhr

James Cone in *The Cross and the Lynching Tree* speaks again to the fundamental message of his theological work: how to reconcile the gospel message of liberation with Black oppression.[25] Within this framework, his central question is: "How could whites confess and live the Christian faith and impose three-and-a-half centuries of slavery and oppression on black people?"[26] This was the deconstructive aspect of his work on white supremacy, and yet there was also a constructive aspect: the revelation of Black religion as the main reality of how "powerless blacks could endure and resist the brutality of white supremacy in nearly every aspect of their lives and still keep their sanity."[27] Specifically, he concluded it was the "immanent presence of a transcendent revelation,"[28] the victorious gospel of Jesus Christ evidenced in the theology of the cross, a Roman lynching, that was liberation and liberative for humanity and the Black church.

In *The Cross and the Lynching Tree*, Cone grapples with the precise challenge of how white Christians could lynch Black people and not make

---

25. James H. Cone, *The Cross and the Lynching Tree*, 2nd printing (New York: Orbis Press, 2012).

26. Cone, *The Cross and the Lynching Tree*, xvii.

27. Cone, *The Cross and the Lynching Tree*, xviii.

28. Cone, *The Cross and the Lynching Tree*, xviii.

71

any obvious connection to the Roman lynching of Jesus and the cross of Christ that they so viscerally proclaimed. In the second chapter, "The Terrible Beauty of the Cross and the Tragedy of the Lynching Tree," Cone says:

> In the "lynching era" between 1880 to 1940, white Christians lynched nearly five thousand black men and women in a manner with obvious echoes of the Roman crucifixion of Jesus. Yet these "Christians" did not see the irony or contradiction in their actions.[29]

It is clear to Cone how the connection of lynching to Calvary would elude white supremacist Christians, but how does one make sense of even the most progressive of white theologians' and thinkers' inability to make this connection? He then takes up Niebuhr, who wrote on many occasions of the suffering and discrimination visited upon Black people. Also, one of the central themes of Niebuhr's work was the cross of Christ. "Christianity," Niebuhr wrote, "is a faith which takes us through tragedy to beyond tragedy, by way of the cross to victory in the cross."[30] All these factors combined to astound Cone that Niebuhr did not make the connection between the cross and the lynching tree, even though lynching was a regular occurrence while Niebuhr was writing and developing his theology. Cone says that, despite all of Niebuhr's brilliance, he missed the most obvious "symbolic re-enactment of the crucifixion in his own time," the lynching of black people.[31] Cone says this "defect in the conscience of white Christians" suggests "why African Americans have needed to trust and cultivate their own theological imagination."[32]

Parenthetically, one exception to Cone's critique would be Clarence Jordan, who in the late 1960s turned his attention more to speaking and writing, specifically his *Cotton Patch* series. It was important to translate not only the words, but also the context of the scriptures. White, but not

---

29. Cone, *The Cross and the Lynching Tree*, 30–31.
30. Reinhold Niebuhr, *Christianity and Power Politics* (New York: Charles Scribner's, 1940), 213.
31. Cone, *The Cross and the Lynching Tree*, 38.
32. Cone, *The Cross and the Lynching Tree*, 32.

a white supremacist Christian, Jordan converted all references to "crucifixion" into references of "lynching":

> [T]here just isn't any word in our vocabulary which adequately translates the Greek word for "crucifixion." *Our* crosses are so shined, so polished, so respectable that to be impaled on one of them would seem to be a blessed experience. We have thus emptied the term "crucifixion" of its original content of terrific emotion, of violence, of indignity and stigma, of defeat. I have translated it as "lynching," well aware that this is not technically correct. Jesus was officially tried and legally condemned, elements generally lacking in a lynching. But having observed the operation of Southern "justice," and at times having been its victim, I can testify that more people have been lynched "by judicial action" than by unofficial ropes. Pilate at least had the courage and the honesty to publicly wash his hands and disavow all legal responsibility. "See to it yourselves," he told the mob. And they did. They crucified him in Judea and they strung him up in Georgia, with a noose tied to a pine tree.[33]

Cone argues that Niebuhr had "a complex perspective on race—at once honest and ambivalent, radical and moderate."[34] Cone recounts multiple examples of Niebuhr's complex perspective, but in the interest of space and time, I recount two. First, Cone quotes Niebuhr: "in the matter of race, we are only a little better than the Nazis," which is honest and radical, and on the other hand Niebuhr urges sympathy for white parents in the South who are opposed to unsegregated schools, which is moderate and ambivalent.[35] Niebuhr says, "if the white man were to expiate his sins committed against the darker races, few white men would have a right to live" (honest and radical), and yet says that the founding fathers were "virtuous and honorable men, and certainly no villains. They merely bowed to the need for establishing national unity based upon a common race and common language" (moderate and ambivalent).[36] During the decade when Willie McGee (1951), Emmett Till (1955), M. C. "Mack" Parker

---

33. Clarence Jordan, "Introduction to Cotton Patch Version of Paul's Epistles," *The Cotton Patch Gospel* (Macon, GA: Smyth & Helwys, 2004), xvii.

34. Cone, *The Cross and the Lynching Tree*, 38.

35. Cone, *The Cross and the Lynching Tree*, 38.

36. Cone, *The Cross and the Lynching Tree*, 38.

(1959), and other Blacks were lynched, rather than listen to civil rights leaders like Martin Luther King Jr., Niebuhr listened to William Faulkner and Hooding Carter, who counseled to "go slow and pause for a moment" in a form of gradualism of change from white liberals, whom King called out in his "Letter from a Birmingham Jail." Cone says Niebuhr identified more with white moderates in the South than with their Black victims, suggesting that it is easy to ask Blacks to go slow and endure a form of oppression that Faulkner, Carter, or Niebuhr would themselves never tolerate.[37]

Cone cites numerous examples of Niebuhr's complex perspective on race, but what accounts for it? Cone suggests that it takes a tremendous amount of empathetic effort to walk in the shoes of African Americans and see the world through their eyes. Cone notes that it has always been difficult for white people to fully empathize with the Black experience, but it has never been impossible. He mentions German theologian Dietrich Bonhoeffer and his work at Abyssinia Baptist Church in Harlem (1930–31) as an example of empathy with Black suffering. Cone mentions Niebuhr's "long love affair with Jewish people and their suffering," but finds strong empathy with Black suffering lacking. Niebuhr preserved class solidarity at the expense of racial justice. Finally, Cone concludes that Niebuhr could have learned more by dialogue with Martin Luther King Jr., James Baldwin, Malcolm X, or other Black thinkers who engaged and urged a more radical discourse and action around issues of Black oppression. In the end, Christian realism was a source of not only Niebuhr's radicalism, but also his conservatism.

Cone closes the chapter by crediting Niebuhr for—in Cone's own discussion of love, power, and justice—helping him to understand that moral suasion alone would never convince whites to relinquish white supremacy; only Black power could do that. Cone says his understanding of the cross is deeply influenced by Niebuhr's perspective on the cross. Niebuhr said the cross of Christ worked a "transvaluation of values." God reveals evil for what it is in the cross, and exalts the suffering of people. Cone also says: Let us likewise see the lynching tree as a "transvaluation of

---

37. Cone, *The Cross and the Lynching Tree*, 39.

values."[38] Cone lauds Niebuhr's intellectual brilliance and creative social ethics based in the cross, but questions his limited perspective, as a white man, on the race crisis in America. Finally, Cone sums up his argument, stating that whites could claim a Christian identity without feeling a contradiction and the need to oppose slavery, segregation, or lynching:

> Whether we speak of Jonathan Edwards, Walter Rauschenbusch, or Reinhold Niebuhr as America's greatest theologian, none of them made the rejection of white supremacy central to their understanding of the gospel. Reinhold Niebuhr could write and preach about the cross with profound theological imagination and say nothing of how the violence of white supremacy invalidated the faith of white churches. It takes a lot of theological blindness to do that, especially since the vigilantes were white Christians who claimed to worship the Jew lynched in Jerusalem. What is invisible to white Christians and their theologians is inescapable to black people.[39]

Cone thought Niebuhr's theology and ethics, as with all white theologians, needed to be informed by a critical reading and dialogue with radical Black perspectives. Just as Martin Luther King Jr. learned much from Niebuhr, Niebuhr could have learned much from Martin Luther King Jr.

Trapped in the Racial Paradigm

Sanjek's global racial hierarchy clarifies how deeply entrenched and trapped all of us are in the 1400s European hierarchy of races, cultures, and religions. The racial hierarchy of white supremacy has done devastating harm and has "transformed and deformed," the life courses and psyches of both its victims and beneficiaries. Cone suggested that Niebuhr had a complex perspective on race—at once honest and ambivalent, radical and moderate. I wonder if that is true not only for Niebuhr, but in reality many of us. Cone says that Niebuhr had such a complex relationship with race because he could not engender true sympathy for the conditions Black Americans suffered. I believe Cone is correct, but I also want to add

---

38. Cone, *The Cross and the Lynching Tree*, 157.
39. Cone, *The Cross and the Lynching Tree*, 159.

that to truly empathize with African Americans or suffering in people, Niebuhr would have had to give up the benefits of the white racial paradigm, the benefits of white privilege. To give up white supremacy is to engage the difficult project of seeking a suitable replacement to the prestige of being better and more superior. Many simply refuse to see the destructive effects on others and find it hard to give up the privilege.

Just as it was hard for Niebuhr to give up the benefits of his status, so might it be with us. For example, let's look at something as simple as a "comfortable" retirement. Many of us have a fear of not having enough money to retire. Many have retirement funds invested in the stock market in some form, and thus the stock market going up relieves the anxiety of not having enough to retire. I have this complex relationship because I write against unbridled capitalism, greed, and the foolishness of a trillion-dollar tax cut to corporations and the wealthy (honest and radical), and yet that tax cut accrues benefit to me in my retirement account while many suffer (ambivalent and moderate). This is perhaps a very simple and possibly trite example, but my point is that the struggle against white supremacy and the capitalism that goes hand in hand with it is very nuanced. Would I be willing to give up the benefits of white supremacy? Does that mean giving up the benefits of my retirement account?

Clarence Jordan, as quoted in the introduction to this book, raised the critical question for us all: "Will you be true to your convictions or will you sell out for your business? . . . For Jesus said, 'Except a man take up his cross and follow me, he cannot be my disciple.'"[40] Not enough of us take up our cross, and that might be why some have so much and others have so very little.

---

40. "Clarence Jordan Tells the Koinonia Story," https://www.youtube.com/watch?v=2g1Z-v-TpI0&feature=emb_rel_end.

Section Two

CLOSE READINGS OF A UNIVERSAL AND TRIBAL GOD

ABRAHAM LINCOLN'S MORAL IMAGINATION: SLAVERY, RACE, AND RELIGION IN THE SECOND INAUGURAL ADDRESS

[T]he most remarkable thing about him [Lincoln] was his tremendous power of growth. He grew in sympathy, in the breath of his humanness, as he grew in other aspects of his mind and spirit. . . . Lincoln's capacity for growth and change helps reconcile those conflicting images of Lincoln—a racist to some and a champion of civil rights for others: the one view reflects the position he started from, the other position he was moving toward.

—David Herbert Donald

There are seminal figures in human history who are so morally imaginative that year after year, decade after decade, century after century, their actions, writings, reflections, beliefs, and practices stir massive human inquiry and interest. It is the moral imagination and the ethical generativity of their wisdom, truth, meanings, symbols, words, actions, and deeds, particularly in a time of threat, crisis, and chaos that their memory and legacy so resonate with and resound to the human family. In the two preceding books of this trilogy, I defined moral imagination as *the ability, intuitive or otherwise, in the midst of the chaotic experiences of human life and existence, to grasp and share abiding wisdom and ethical truth to benefit the individual and common humanity.* I also defined the anti-moral or diabolical imagination as that which *delights in death, destruction, cynicism, despair, the subhuman and the perverse and panders to the lust for violence, devastation, cruelty, and sensational disorder.* While much of this is standard fare in pornography, prime-time television, Hollywood scripts, and the commercial airwaves that result in the drowning of innocence, there are figures that are so destructive of human life that their evil captivates, astounds, and merits further attention and study, if for no other reason than to prevent such malevolence from ever happening again.

Many of the chaotic experiences of human existence result from this ever-present human dilemma: how do individuals, especially in groups—families, clans, factions, political parties, religious persuasions, nations, and states—live together when we are different in religion, culture, politics, interests, and values? How do we overcome the human tendency to violence, mobs and riots, hate, oppression, destruction, greed, cruelty, discrimination, domination, war, rape, and pillage in the face of human difference? How do we operate out of the moral rather than diabolical imagination?

Certain seminal individuals from every walk of life, based in their moral imaginations, have injected new meanings of reconciliation, justice, and peace to overcome the racism, nativism, tribalism, nationalism, bigotry, misogyny and sexism, homophobia, and xenophobia so omnipresent in the human community. These inspirational figures are written about and explored from sundry fields and angles of thought and reflection. As a Christian, I believe *the* seminal figure of moral imagination in human history to be Jesus the Christ.

An American seminal figure led our nation through the Civil War of 1861–1865, the greatest threat to the American experiment the nation has ever known. More than a century and a half since his tragic death, the interest in and publication about Abraham Lincoln continues unabated. Lincoln grappled intensely with several of the most pernicious, pervasive, and persistent moral issues of the American experiment: slavery, race, and religion. The constellation of these issues expressed themselves in secession from the Union by the South, the resulting civil war, and, finally, the reconstruction of the nation after the North at long last prevailed. Based in the vast death and destruction that ensued, Lincoln sought to give the war meaning by clarifying its cause and the Christian God's role and purpose. In summary of this enormous moral struggle, religion historian Harry S. Stout labeled Lincoln "the martyred prophet . . . the theologian of reconciliation."[1] Lincoln attempted to chart an imaginative course for the nation by responding to the moral question: what does it mean to live together after violence, war, and unparalleled death with justice, reconciliation, peace, and forgiveness?

Undoubtedly, some of the fascination has been that Lincoln's life was cut short by an assassin's bullet. There was a near deification of Lincoln by many, especially in the African American community, which labeled Lincoln "Father Abraham," "the Great Emancipator," and the like. The fact that Lincoln was shot on Good Friday added to the sense that God had ordained his life and death. Our goal herein is not to deify or vilify Lincoln, but to explore his example as a flawed human being who in a time of overwhelming crisis grew and developed and was morally imaginative at a profound level. While Lincoln was a conservative thinker before the war, as James Tackach says, "a politically and intellectually cautious man by nature," he had the ability to question his "fixed attitudes on slavery, race, and religion, and other key issues of his time."[2] The result was significant personal growth and transformation, and the enlargement of his moral imagination. Many scholars have identified this capacity for self-examination and growth as one of Lincoln's most remarkable traits. David Herbert Donald suggests that Lincoln's enormous capacity for growth

enabled one of the least experienced and most poorly prepared men ever elected to high office to become the greatest American President. Richard

---

1. Harry S. Stout, "Abraham Lincoln as Moral Leader: The Second Inaugural as America's Sermon to the World," from *Lincoln and Leadership: Military, Political, and Religious Decision Making*, ed. Randall M. Miller (New York: Fordham University Press, 2012), 79.

2. James Tackach, *Lincoln's Moral Vision: The Second Inaugural Address* (Jackson: University of Mississippi Press, 2002), xxii.

N. Current concurs: "[T]he most remarkable thing about him [Lincoln] was his tremendous power of growth. He grew in sympathy, in the breath of his humaneness, as he grew in other aspects of his mind and spirit." . . . Lincoln's capacity for growth and change helps reconcile those conflicting images of Lincoln—a racist to some and a champion of civil rights for others: "The one view reflects the position he started from, the other the position he was moving toward."[3]

Lincoln's massive growth and transformation in the midst of the moral dilemmas of slavery, race, and religion makes him relevant today. America is still grappling with virtually the same issues: slavery in the form of institutionalized racism, race in the form of racial equality, and religion in the form of whose religious beliefs can dominate the public square. The same need for moral imagination exists today. This motivates me to study Lincoln's life, thoughts, and for our purposes herein, theology and rhetoric. I want to look at Lincoln's moral imagination as expressed in the Second Inaugural Address and, specifically, the God of the Dangerous Sermon behind that address. Through a close reading of the address, I hope to demonstrate that out of his moral imagination Lincoln proclaimed a living, just, and universal God of healing and reconciliation rather than a tribal God of sectionalism and factionalism.

Let me respond to a question that might be lingering in the minds of many readers: how can a study of a presidential address be positioned in a homiletics textbook? Underneath this first question might be a second question: how does the study of a political speech make one a better preacher?

First, the rhetorical theology that I seek to define herein studies all "sacred rhetoric." Sacred rhetoric is any form of oratory wherein the speaker uses language and/or symbols of God in the attempt to address or persuade an audience. The orator is appealing to a God who can be characteristically discerned by a rhetorical read of the very language, symbols, metaphors, and the speaker's call to action. The speaker summons the audience to imitate and become like this God. This reflection on sacred rhetoric helps us as preachers to carefully think through and discern the

---

3. Tackach, *Lincoln's Moral Vision*, xiii.

language, symbols, and metaphors that we utilize when we preach and the God we are appealing to and asking the congregation to imitate in our sermons. Any oration that makes God claims or appeals to a God is worthy of study by any adherent of rhetorical theology.

Second, many scholars agree that the Second Inaugural was a sermon in all but name. At a reception at the White House following it, Lincoln asked Frederick Douglass for his opinion of the speech. Douglass replied, "Mr. Lincoln, that was a sacred effort." Later Douglass explained, "the address sounded more like a sermon than a state paper."[4] Stout remarks, "like Martin Luther King Jr.'s 'I Have a Dream' speech, the cadences, phraseology, biblical illusions, and deep moral stirrings bespeak more the pulpit than the podium."[5] Stout compares the Second Inaugural to what he regards as America's greatest sermon, Jonathan Edwards's "Sinners in the Hands of an Angry God." Several other scholars agree that, though Lincoln was not a preacher, the Second Inaugural is a sermon to the nation and the world.

Third, as Stout astutely picks up, in the study of the Second Inaugural, scholars have missed how closely Lincoln upheld the sermonic form of the Puritan jeremiad sermon. For a more detailed discussion of the Puritan, American, African American, and secular Jeremiad, please review my discussion in *American Dream 2.0.*[6]

Rhetorical Analysis of the Second Inaugural

By the time of the Second Inaugural, March 4, 1865, Lincoln was a beleaguered president. While he had been lambasted by critics in Congress and the press for much of the war, he would offer this Second Inaugural with his leadership vindicated by victory in the field. He was beginning to

---

4. Stout, "Abraham Lincoln as Moral Leader," 78.

5. Stout, "Abraham Lincoln as Moral Leader," 78–79.

6. Frank A. Thomas, "The American Jeremiad and the Cultural Myth of America" in *American Dream 2.0: A Christian Way Out of the Great Recession* (Nashville: Abingdon Press, 2012), 3–15.

receive praise and credit. Because Lincoln believed the South never legally seceded from the Union, he advocated for forgiveness and "reconstruction." In 1863, Lincoln issued the Proclamation of Amnesty and Reconstruction, which openly declared his determination to reunify the North and South. Lincoln hoped that the proclamation would rally Northern support for the war and persuade weary Confederate soldiers to surrender. Lincoln's allowance of colored soldiers to fight in the Union Army and the 1863 Emancipation Proclamation brought coloreds, free and slave, to the Union cause in droves. Ultimately they were vital in helping the North to win the war. By 1865, it was clear that the United States government and the Union Army had all but prevailed. It was not personal vindication that Lincoln was after, but the Union and reunification. The moral vision of one democratic nation again consumed his heart, passion, and purpose as a leader. A president singularly and uncompromisingly committed to the purpose of preserving the Union penned the Second Inaugural address to begin to heal the wounds of the nation.

Lincoln had before him a difficult task requiring the heights and depths of the growth and transformation of his moral imagination. Losses from war were taking a huge toll on families everywhere; an estimated 623,000 people died in the Civil War. The death of so many fathers, brothers, husbands, and sons on both sides garnered incalculable grief. What did victory and defeat mean in the shadow of so costly and great a tragedy? Would the president advocate for immediate implementation of Reconstruction? What about the four million slaves who were now "free"? What would be done concerning the matter of their suffrage? Would they now be full American citizens? Would Lincoln offer a triumphant victory speech castigating the South for its recalcitrance and the sin of slavery? Would he really follow through on reconstruction and forgiveness, or were the Confederates to be treated as a conquered nation? Would the Confederacy's civic and military leaders be charged with treason? Or was there some other vision or course the president would set for the nation? Without question, there was wide interest, speculation, and concern as to exactly what Abraham Lincoln would say.

I have divided the speech into three movements, the first "No prediction is ventured," the second "All dreaded it—all sought to avert it," and the final "malice toward none; with charity for all."

Movement One: "No prediction is ventured"

Lincoln begins the speech in subdued and somber tones with the term "Fellow Countrymen." His purpose is to discuss the deeper moral cause and meaning of the war, but to move to such depth of thought, he has to re-set audience expectation. He is clear in this first movement as to what the speech is not, in order to set up the deeper conversation. He changes audience expectation by using the qualifying language of *less*, *little*, and *no*. He says, at this "second appearing" [Second Inaugural] there is "*less* occasion for an extended address than there was at the first [Inaugural]."[7] So much had been said that "*little* that is new that could be presented about the great contest." The nation had talked about the war ad infinitum in the last four years and he could not add anything new to the discussion. Therefore, in contradistinction to vast audience expectation, the speech would offer *no* information on the war per se. Also, given the fact that victory for the North seemed imminent, there would be no discussion of restoring the nation on the Union's exclusive terms: no revelry, triumphalism, or celebration of victory, and especially no discussion of treason and punishment for the South. Lincoln offered no specific policy proposals and platitudes about the greatness of America and its government. This was to be a very different inaugural than the traditional and standard inaugural speech.

Again, Lincoln wants to discuss national issues of great moral struggle, such as what did God demand of the nation that Lincoln called "the last best hope of humankind"? How does the nation make sense of the slaughter and suffering other than simplistic civic and religious explanations of scapegoating the other side? How does the nation give these great sacrifices of loss and death meaning? These are moral issues that require use of imagination, the moral imagination. Lincoln's Second Inaugural is

---

7. All quoted references are from "Lincoln's Second Inaugural," U.S. Department of the Interior, https://www.nps.gov/linc/learn/historyculture/lincoln-second-inaugural.htm.

an attempt to shape the moral imagination and behavior of the nation by articulation of a theology of reconciliation based in his understanding of a universal God, the Supreme Ruler of the nations, who paid close attention to the American experiment and punished America severely for its offence of slavery. But, in the raw optimism of the American jeremiad, judgment and punishment was not the final word. Lincoln offered the nation a new and healing future for all parties involved regardless of the past.

The conversation that Lincoln was seeking to have with the nation and the world was the conversation that he had been having deep inside his own soul, expressed to this point only in private, and in the Second Inaugural for the first time in a public address. The war had gone on far longer and at a cost far higher than either side could have planned for or predicted. He ends the first paragraph and movement of the address with the statement that "with high hopes for the future," in regards to the war, "*no* prediction in regard to it is ventured."

Movement Two: "All dreaded it; all sought to avert it"

The second movement of the speech begins with a reference to the First Inaugural when Lincoln says, "all thoughts were anxiously directed to an impending civil war." Notice this is his first utilization of the term "civil war" as opposed to "great contest" in the first paragraph. He clearly begins to outline his strategy for holding the nation together. He cannot paper over the reality that the nation is at war with itself. He says, "All dreaded it—all sought to avert it." He uses *all,* and its surrogates, *both, each, neither, American,* and *toward none* to convey that the nation is one with a painful and tragic difference of opinion. Despite the violence and the bloodshed of war, the nation is not two separate peoples, necessitating language of us vs. them or North vs. South. Speaking of the civil war, he says, "*All* dreaded it—*all* sought to avert it." Lincoln's use of the word *all* and its surrogates in his language structure is symbolic of his great struggle to hold North and South together in legal, material, and spiritual reality. His language attempts to hold the nation together even as his actions do the same. Though he recognizes the division, he is not using the language of division.

His phraseology of *all* has the connotation of not only holding both sides together, but also holding them together in tension. He says that while the First Inaugural address was being devoted to saving the union without war, "insurgents" were in the city at that very time seeking to destroy the Union without war. He labels them "insurgents" who were seeking to dissolve the Union and divide the "effects" of the nation through a process of negotiation. The "all" of which Lincoln speaks is fraught with the tensions of division and difference visible in the tangible behavior of both sides in regards to the war. He continues to hold North and South in tension by stating that while *both* (a derivative of all) parties deprecated war, one of them [the South] would make war rather than let the nation survive, and the other [the North] would accept war rather than let it perish. Lincoln is clear that the *all* of which he speaks is not an idyllic *all* of harmony and good feelings, but the togetherness of a family with tension, strife, and violence.

After holding *both* sides in tension, Lincoln makes a potent statement, and a shift in preoccupation away from human actions, perspectives, and behaviors indicated by this phrase, "And the war came." He does not say the South or the North brought the war. He does not blame either side, but is careful to say, "the war came." Lincoln is suggesting that, for all the aggressive language and argument, neither side was fully in control. Ronald C. White, Jr. in his book *Lincoln's Greatest Speech: The Second Inaugural*, suggests that Lincoln looked back from the perspective of four long years and saw that, all along, the war had a life of its own. White quotes Charles Royster, who says with the scale of destruction to which the participants committed themselves to in the Civil War, "Americans surprised themselves with the extent of violence they could attain."[8] Lincoln concluded that though there were battle plans and projections, arguments and actions, in the moral and spiritual arena participants had battled in total confusion. For Lincoln, reason alone could not explain the bloodshed and violence because the level of death and destruction had grown incomprehensible. Independent of presidents, generals, soldiers, and populations,

---

8. Ronald C. White, Jr., *Lincoln's Greatest Speech: The Second Inaugural* (New York: Simon and Schuster, 2002), 78.

the war had a life of its own. White says that at this point in the speech, "War becomes the subject and is no longer a direct object of the action of others."[9] Lincoln now moves to discuss the direct cause of the war.

Although in the First Inaugural the purpose of the impending war was to preserve the Union, nevertheless, after four long years of war, it is clear to Lincoln that the cause of the war has shifted. Lincoln introduces slaves into the address as one-eighth of the population, mostly situated in the South. He defines them as a "peculiar and powerful [economic] interest." He returns to the subject of *all*: "*All* knew that this interest was *somehow* the cause of the war." The word *somehow* is very significant in that it suggests a sense of mystery on both sides as to how slavery became the cause of the war. Lincoln will later unfold the source of *somehow* as the hand and providence of God.

Lincoln states that the objective of the insurgents was to strengthen, perpetuate, and extend this economic interest by rending the Union even by war, while the government only wanted to restrict territorial enlargement of slavery. Notice the tension of the language of insurgents and the government. Lincoln then reverts back to holding everyone together in tension:

> *Neither* party expected for the war the magnitude or the duration. . . . *Neither* anticipated that the cause of the conflict might cease with or even before the conflict itself should cease. *Each* looked for an easier triumph and a result less fundamental and astounding. *Both* read the same Bible and pray to the same God and each invokes His aid against the other.

Neither party could anticipate the magnitude of duration of the war, nor that the initial cause for the war would be transformed. In human terms, as White says, "Lincoln was driven to the alternative of either surrendering the Union, and with it the Constitution, or of arming Southern slaves."[10] According to Lincoln's plan, the Union would be preserved first, and then the slaves would be freed. *Somehow*, a hint at divine initiative, the second step had become the first step. He returns to the sense of *all*.

9. White, *Lincoln's Greatest Speech*, 12.

10. White, *Lincoln's Greatest Speech*, 82.

Each side in their human interest had looked for an easier triumph. *Both sides* read the same Bible, prayed to the same God, and invoked God's aid against the other. While *both sides* were certain of their own righteousness, Lincoln is setting up the reality of divine punishment and purposes rather than human plans and outcomes.

Lincoln then makes a major shift and unfolds in theological detail the true cause of the war. Lincoln quotes Genesis 3:19, where Adam and Eve had sinned, and, because of their sin, God tells Adam, "in the sweat of thy face shalt thou eat." Lincoln asks the question: How is it that anyone could ask a just God to assist in "wringing their bread from the sweat of other men's faces?" He is challenging slavery as against the biblical mandate of Genesis 3:19 (KJV). He lets the judgment linger momentarily on the South, whom most of the audience would think that he is exclusively referring to. He then quickly flips audience expectation and quotes Matthew 7:1, where Jesus in the Sermon on the Mount says, "Let us not judge, lest we be judged" (KJV). Many in the North wanted to judge, and had already judged, but he is telling them to be careful because in fact they will be under the same judgment. He is guarding against self-righteousness by those of the North, because the truth is the North had complicity in slavery. Lincoln is not interested in a tribal God who is on the side of the North or the South and who would punish one side over the other.

Because God is not a tribal God, the prayers of *both sides* against the other could not be answered and *neither side's* prayer had been fully answered because "the Almighty has his own purposes." God's purposes are something different than that of either party. Lincoln then slips back to judgment, "Woe unto the world because of offences! for it must needs be that offences come; but woe to that man by whom the offence cometh!" He is quoting Jesus in Matthew 18:3-7 (KJV):

> Except ye be converted, and become as little children, ye shall not enter into the kingdom of heaven. . . . But whoso shall offend one of these little ones which believe in me, it were better for him that a millstone were hanged about his neck. . . . Woe unto the world because of offences! for it must needs be that offence come, but woe to the man by whom the offence cometh.

89

Lincoln is making plain that slavery is the offence and the little ones be-ing offended are slave populations. Slavery is one of the offences, which in God's providence must come, and will continue until God's appointed time. Lincoln surmises that God wills to remove *American* slavery (an-other term of *all*), and, as a result, has given the North and the South "this terrible war" as a woe for the offence. Notice, as a sign of *all*, Lincoln calls it *American* slavery and not Southern slavery. Lincoln then suggests that slavery does not line up with any attributes "which the believers in a Liv-ing God always ascribe to Him." In other words, slavery cannot be consis-tent with any attribute of a Living God. Lincoln offers hope and prayer:

> Fondly do we hope—fervently do we pray—that this mighty scourge of war may speedily pass away. Yet, if God wills that it continue until all the wealth piled . . . by two hundred and fifty years of unrequited toil shall be sunk and until every drop of blood drawn with the lash shall be paid by the sword, as was said three thousand years ago, so still it must be said, "the judgments of the Lord, are true and righteous altogether."

Notice the use of the word *scourge*, chastisement or punishment, most notably used in Hebrews 12:6: "for whom the Lord loves he chas-tens, and scourges every son whom He receives" (NKJV). Slavery has been harsh and the nation's sin has been severe, so severe that, as Tack-ach paraphrases Lincoln's meaning: "the war's losses were the wages of national sin, payable in both life and treasure."[11] Lincoln fully assents and submits to God's judgment, quoting Psalm 19:7–9 (KJV), "The judgments of the Lord are true and righteous altogether." In this sec-ond movement, the theme is *all*: *both* the North and South were being judged for the offence of slavery. Though *each side*, in serving their tribal God, blames, finds fault, and prays against the other, God is not on ei-ther side. God is not a tribal God.

Even in the pronouncement, of judgment, consistent with the tone and tenor of the American jeremiad, Lincoln is after reconciliation. It would not serve the cause of reconciliation if the South were burdened with the singular guilt of the war. The North was complicit as well.

---

11. Tackach, *Lincoln's Moral Vision*, 138.

Tackach explains the complicity in great detail as the South cultivating slavery and the North tolerating it for its own advantage:

> Thomas Jefferson's original draft of the Declaration of Independence charged King George III for waging, "a cruel war against human nature itself, violating its most sacred right of life and Liberty in the persons of a distant people who never offended him, captivating them into slavery in another hemisphere, or to incur miserable death in their transportation thither." When the representatives from the Southern slaveholding colonies protested this passage, these words were struck from the Declaration. For the sake of unity against Great Britain, the Northern colonies acquiesced to the South's peculiar institution. Again for the sake of unity, the delegates at the Philadelphia convention of 1787 chose not to create a Constitution that outlawed slavery. The Northern textile mills spun Southern cotton picked by slaves. White laborers in the border states like Indiana and Lincoln's Illinois relied on slavery to keep the Blacks out, assuring the jobs would be available for white workers and that pay scales would not fall. To preserve the union, antislavery Northerners like Daniel Webster compromised with the slave power, passing the Fugitive Slave Law and other legislation that protected slavery.[12]

The South had been articulating Northern complicity for generations. While many did not, Lincoln had the moral capacity to see that *both* North and South participated in slavery. Because of this moral capacity, Lincoln never spoke about God in the language of triumphalism. He was very suspicious of church leaders who knew exactly when, where, and how God was on their side. The bottom line was that Lincoln did not see himself as exclusively a Northern president; he was the president of the North and South.

For my purposes, the God of the Dangerous Sermon is the God revealed in Lincoln's Second Inaugural. These are the attributes of God that can be discerned from the address.

- a Living God, not a tribal or territorial God, choosing one party in the conflict over the other;

- an inclusive God, a universal God offering both judgment and reconciliation;

---

12. Tackach, *Lincoln's Moral Vision*, 136.

- a God of covenant evidenced in a relationship with America similar to that with the Hebrew nation of the Old Testament;

- a God of mercy revealed and evidenced in Jesus and his Sermon on the Mount;

- a God of evenhanded justice of the entire human race, especially those with favored status;

- a providential God whose purposes are not fully known and who is active in orchestrating human affairs towards mysterious ends;

- a God not as concerned for individual salvation per se, but for the nation as a collective;

- a God not as concerned with the theological doctrine of damnation in the afterlife, but with hell on earth;

- a God concerned for the "little ones" and the offences they receive.

Lincoln wrote to Eliza Gurney in 1862:

We must believe that He permits it [the war] for some wise purpose of his own, mysterious and unknown to us; and though with our limited understandings we may not be able to comprehend it, yet we cannot but believe that he who made the world still governs it.[13]

Lincoln fully reveals the God of the universe, the Supreme Ruler of all nations, who holds nations and people accountable but also offers mercy, love, and reconciliation if the nations and people would accept it and act in peace and reconciliation with each other. Lincoln then explains the ethics of the Living God.

Movement Three: "With malice toward none; with charity for all"

The distinguishing factor of the American jeremiad is its optimism and hope. God in mercy in the midst of judgment ultimately offers

13. White, *Lincoln's Greatest Speech*, 142.

redemption to America. Lincoln, out of his moral imagination, based in the mercy and grace of the Living God, paints a post–Civil War vision of America:

> With malice *toward none*; with charity for *all*; with firmness in the right, as God gives us to see the right, let us strive on to finish the work we are in: to bind up the nation's wounds; to care for him who shall have borne the battle, and for his widow and his orphan—to do all which may achieve and cherish a just and a lasting peace among ourselves, and with all the nations.

Lincoln holds the nation together, resolves the tension of difference, and charts a future of forgiveness and reconciliation for *all*. To overcome the desire to punish and garner revenge on the South and to deal with the South's anger and humiliation at being defeated, he suggests malice toward none. Malice is not simply evil, it is directed evil with the intent to harm and hurt. Lincoln believes malice is the ethic of a tribal God. The universal and inclusive God offers charity for *all*. Lincoln is not simply talking about unselfish love among like neighbors of the same tribe, family, party, or clan, but Jesus's radical ethic of agape love for enemies. This vision is based in a God of reconciliation and forgiveness who had been the principal actor in the Civil War. Lincoln is calling the nation to overcome the boundaries of race, regionalism, political parties, and sectarian policies to come together in reconciliation and forgiveness. Despite judgment, Lincoln believed that the Living God, who has divine, not human purposes, would renew and restore the nation back to the covenant.

Lincoln says "with firmness in the right, as God gives us to see the right." He is emphasizing the severe limitation of human righteousness. He was weary and wary of leaders, and especially church leaders, who knew that God was on their side. He had seen firsthand the harm caused by those who were absolutely sure that their purposes were right and they were acting for God. Lincoln struggled with the lack of humility in the moral lives of so many of the principal actors in the civil conflict—the hypocrisy and moral pretentiousness of those who wanted to punish the South as if the North was not complicit, and the self-righteous ministers and churches on both sides with biblical justifications of unimaginable suffering—and yet no sense that they were contributing to and making the violence possible.

Basic in the ethic of the Living God, Lincoln makes very specific appeals to finish the nation's work: "to bind up the nation's wounds; to care for him who shall have borne the battle, and for his widow and his orphan." Starting with soldiers who bore the battle and their families, so many of whom had become widows and orphans, Lincoln called forth compassion and mercy as the true test of whether the nation understood the purposes of God in the war. It was not just victory, but how one treated those who were defeated that God was careful to observe. If hostilities continued after the war and neither side learned anything, then the war would have been for naught.

Lincoln concludes with: "to do *all* which may achieve and cherish a just and lasting peace among ourselves and with *all* nations." Stout says that Lincoln believed passionately in the U.S. republic. It was his "political religion," one he hoped would be preached to the world:

> But it was not nationalism for the sake of nationalism. . . . Lincoln's was a prudential and moral nationalism. Put simply, he would have never said, "my country right or wrong." The United States, Lincoln believed, deserved reverential awe only to the extent it conformed to the higher ethical imperative contained in the principle that "all men are created equal." That is why he said repeatedly that the nation could not survive only "half slave and half free," including the territories and States in waiting, that it was a Republic not worth preserving.[14]

In summary, Lincoln believed the nation had sinned in the development, perpetuation, and tolerance of slavery. *All* had offended God, and God gave the "scourge" of war as corrective punishment. God offered redemption and a new path for the nation—malice toward none, binding up the nation's wounds, to care for those who have borne the battle and their widows and orphans, and to do everything to achieve a just and lasting peace, among Americans and with all nations.

---

14. Stout, "Abraham Lincoln as Moral Leader," 92.

Responses to the Second Inaugural

Without a comprehensive amount of detailed analysis, given time and space, suffice it to say that generally the responses of citizens and newspapers to the address were mixed. As could be predicted, pro-Republican newspapers praised the speech, while Democrat-leaning newspapers chided it, and average citizens were split as well. What is of the most importance for our purposes is what Lincoln said about the speech, and why it had the mixed effect from Lincoln's perspective. After carefully surveying responses to the Second Inaugural, on March 15, 1865, Lincoln said this in a letter to Thurlow Weed, a New York Republican Party supporter:

> I expect the latter, the address, [Second Inaugural] to wear as well as—perhaps better than—anything that I have produced; but I believe it is not immediately popular. Men are not flattered by being shown that there has been a difference of purpose between the Almighty and them. To deny it, however, in this case is to deny that there is a God governing the world. It is a truth which I thought needed to be told; and as whatever of humiliation there is in it, falls most directly on myself, I thought others might afford for me to tell it.[15]

For Lincoln, the response to the speech was perfectly reasonable. Lincoln had considered all of the risks involved in giving such an address and understood that it is very difficult for any people to recognize the evil they perpetrate. We as human beings are very uncomfortable and almost blind to facing up to our own evil. Typically, in conflict or war, all of the evil is projected upon the enemy, the other side. Rather than deal with our own evil, we project it outside of ourselves to some other person, group, or nation. We see ourselves as righteous, and many even equate our purposes with God's purposes and plans.

For Lincoln, if one was not willing to look at, face up to, and admit to one's own evil and complicity with evil, the odds were that if one claimed to be serving God, it was a tribal God. Lincoln believed that North and South served a tribal God, and what he was advocating in the Second Inaugural was a universal God who was just and ferreted out the evil in

---

15.   Library of Congress, https://www.loc.gov/resource/lprbscsm.scsm0823/.

all people and nations, especially a nation that claimed a special and covenant relationship with God. Lincoln did not exclude himself from the same judgment he proclaimed to the nation. He had only recently and reluctantly come to the position of definitively acting to abolish slavery. Lincoln admitted to being complicit. Regardless, like the biblical prophets, the truth had to be told. He took full responsibility, allowing whatever humiliation he would take to fall directly on himself. He thought that despite the difficulty of the humiliation of hearing and learning that God's will and purpose differs from one's own, the nation might give him the chance to say it. He did not expect that it would be popular, but in the sweep of history he expected the address to wear as well as, perhaps better than, any other speech he had produced.

African American Responses to the Second Inaugural

African Americans understood and said openly and clearly what the speech meant to them. In the call and response of African American oral traditions, the African Americans present at the Second Inaugural responded thusly as reported by *The New York Herald*: "After virtually every sentence they offered, 'bress [bless] the Lord.' They offered in call and response 'Amen' to Lincoln's words. Not only did they realize that they were hearing a sermon they had often heard in their churches, but to hear it from the President of the United States had the highest meaning and most solemn impact."[16] It would be similar to the response of Martin Luther King Jr. to President Lyndon Johnson's 1965 announcement of the Voting Rights Act. When Johnson said on national television the mantra of the freedom struggle, "We shall overcome," it is reported that King openly wept. Likewise in 1865 African Americans realized, despite the Emancipation Proclamation of 1863, they were finally hearing what generations of African Americans had wanted to hear from an American president. Richard Carwardine, in *Lincoln: A Life of Purpose and Power*,

---

16. White, *Lincoln's Greatest Speech*, 182.

96

relates an experience that sums up most African American responses to the speech: "At a Fast day gathering near the White House, an old preacher with a voice like a gong prayed with hands uplifted, 'O Lord, command the sun and the moon to stand still, while Joshua Abraham Lincoln fights the battle of freedom.'"[17] For African Americans, Lincoln was obviously being led by the divine will in the manner of the Hebrew prophets and Jesus of Nazareth.

Harry S. Stout articulates what he labels "the central moral paradox animating the speech: Over the whole, African Americans did not share in the complicity of slavery, . . . and therefore could justifiably stand outside the judgment prohibition."[18] Stout points out that slaves in the South and free Blacks in the North were innocent; the evils of slavery were perpetrated *upon* African Americans. Stout says, "though the speech is noble and has moral gravitas, it also has moral limitations, . . . while deeply ethical, it is not the only moral position to take on the issue of judgement."[19] Lincoln held out the promise of reconciliation for northern and southern whites as friends. But what about the free Blacks and slaves, who were not under moral judgement? How were African Americans to be included in the promise of reconciliation as friends?

As we said earlier, Frederick Douglass was complimentary of the speech, but also had strong concerns and deep reservation about its implications for the freedom and citizenship of African Americans. Standing outside of Lincoln's white audience, Douglass thought that "too much forgiveness led to too much acceptance."[20] The result of too much acceptance by the North without any punishment for the South would be enslavement and re-enslavement for Black forced captives by different means. As long as the nation's priority was on the Union and not racial equality, racism would endure and rear its ugly head in another form. Stout quotes Douglass:

---

17. Richard Carwardine, *Lincoln: A Life of Purpose and Power* (New York: Vintage Books, 2003), 279.

18. Stout, "Abraham Lincoln as Moral Leader," 84.

19. Stout, "Abraham Lincoln as Moral Leader," 82.

20. Stout, "Abraham Lincoln as Moral Leader," 84.

The law and the sword cannot abolish the malignant slaveholding sentiment which has kept the slave system alive in his country during two centuries. Pride of race, prejudice against color, will raise their hateful clamor
for oppression of the Negro as heretofore. The slave having ceased to be the
abject slave of a single master, his enemies will endeavor to make him the
slave of society at large.[21]

Of course, history has proved Douglass right. The moral position of
the African American population was racial equality, and ultimately racial
equality was abandoned. For a short time, Reconstruction as an alternative vision of judgment and remaking the South achieved impressive
results for African American equality. Federal troops were placed in the
South to ensure equality, but when Federal troops were removed during
the Compromise of 1877, Blacks were left without protection from the
violence and intimidation of the South again, with complicity from the
North. It was precisely the possibility of the eventual tradeoffs between
North and South with the abandoning of racial equality that led Douglass
to oppose any unpunished reconciliation with the former confederacy.
David Blight, in *Race and Reunion*, points out that the moral imagination
of the majority of white Americans did not allow any real reconciliation
without the re-subjugation of those who had been freed from bondage.
Douglass said that after the government had asked the slaves to "espouse
its cause and turn against [his] master," they were returned to their masters without a single shred of protection.[22] There were moral limitations
on Lincoln's admonition not to judge. Of course, Lincoln did not live to
further flesh out his vision and push the issue of racial equality. And so the
great moral paradox, racial inequality, having infested the heart of American society from the founding of the nation, lingers until today. Racial
equality was and is a moral limitation and lack of moral imagination for
many in America.

Lincoln's leadership is based in an expansive and profound moral
imagination, centered around the Constitution of the United States
and the Bible of Christian faith. Lincoln's God is a God of justice and

---

21. Stout, "Abraham Lincoln as Moral Leader," 84.

22. Stout, "Abraham Lincoln as Moral Leader," 85.

mercy—in the simplest of terms, not a tribal God, but a God of simple acts of kindness to people outside one's group. Lincoln speaks forever and the ages against what White terms "God Bless America" theology.[23] This includes any theology that claims the blessings of God without coming to terms with its own evil and hypocrisy. White says it best, "the peril of theological politics is the danger of self-righteousness."[24]

Lincoln's Final Address and Colored Enfranchisement

On April 9, 1865, General Robert E. Lee formally surrendered and the Civil War was finally over. Now with victory in hand, Lincoln was certain that difficulties lay ahead, because there was no previous blueprint for secession, civil war, or the aftermath. Next steps and directions would be acts of imagination—in my language, moral imagination. Lincoln mandated that for admission back into the Union the South had to accept the Emancipation Proclamation of 1863 and the Thirteenth Amendment to the Constitution, which abolished slavery and involuntary servitude except as a punishment for a crime.

On April 11, 1865, from the north portico of the executive mansion on a muddy and misty night with thousands gathered, Lincoln gave the last public speech of his life. Upon Lincoln's last appearing, he was greeted with overwhelming and continuous applause. Lincoln began, "We meet this evening, not in sorrow, but in gladness of heart. The evacuation of Petersburg and Richmond, and the surrender of the principal insurgent army, give hope of a righteous and speedy peace whose joyous expression cannot be restrained."[25] He immediately gave thanks to God, saying, "He from whom all blessings flow must not be forgotten."[26]

---

23. White, *Lincoln's Greatest Speech*, 203.

24. White, *Lincoln's Greatest Speech*, 203.

25. All quotes from this point are from "Lincoln's Last Public Address," Lincoln Online, http://www.abrahamlincolnonline.org/lincoln/speeches/last.htm.

26. http://www.abrahamlincolnonline.org/lincoln/speeches/last.htm.

Lincoln then turned to the main subject of his speech, which few expected: Reconstruction.

The audience expected celebration and not such weighty moral matters. But Lincoln said, "The re-inauguration of the national authority—reconstruction—which has had a large share of thought from the first, is pressed much more closely upon our attention." Lincoln saw Reconstruction not as a matter to take up upon the end of the war, but an actual means to win the war. On December 8, 1863, he had issued a Proclamation of Amnesty and Reconstruction that provided a plan by which states in rebellion could be reorganized and restored to the nation, once a tenth of eligible voters established a loyal government and adopted a state constitution that abolished slavery.

Lincoln sought to have Louisiana, which had adopted a new constitution, formally restored, but Congress absolutely refused. Lincoln took his argument to the people in this, his last speech. He argued that twelve thousand voters in Louisiana had sworn allegiance to the Union. In their desire to return to the Union, they held an election, organized a state governing, adopted a free state constitution that abolished slavery, and provided for public schooling for Blacks as well as whites. They had even empowered the legislature to confer elective franchise upon the "the colored man," though it had not been enacted to date. Lincoln said no good thing could be accomplished by rejecting the new state government:

> Now, if we reject, and spurn them, we do our utmost to disorganize and disperse them. We in effect say to the white men "You are worthless, or worse—we will neither help you, nor be helped by you." To the blacks we say "This cup of liberty which these, your old masters, hold to your lips, we will dash from you, and leave you to the chances of gathering the spilled and scattered contents in some vague and undefined when, where, and how." If this course, discouraging and paralyzing both white and black, has any tendency to bring Louisiana into proper practical relations with the Union, I have, so far, been unable to perceive it.[27]

This was the first time that Lincoln publicly acknowledged his support for enfranchisement for the "colored man." This was the first statement in

27. http://www.abrahamlincolnonline.org/lincoln/speeches/last.htm.

the nation's history whereby a president endorsed black voting, albeit that Lincoln specifically was talking about the vote for very intelligent Black men and soldiers who had fought in the Union army. Two men in the crowd, Southern sympathizers, were outraged by what they heard. Louis P. Masur says, "John Wilkes Booth tried to persuade Lewis Powell to shoot the president as he stood in the window, but Powell refused to take the chance."[28] At the conclusion of the speech Booth said, "That means Nigger Citizenship. Now by God, I will put him through. That is the last speech he will ever make."[29]

I am certain that "nigger citizenship" was not the only reason John Wilkes Booth killed Lincoln. His motive was more complex, and yet this one factor was so outrageous that it seemed to be the final straw. It must be noted that what Lincoln said in his last speech is exactly what happened: "This cup of liberty which these, your old masters, hold to your lips, we will dash from you, and leave you to the chances of gathering the spilled and scattered contents in some vague and undefined when, where, and how." This is the result of a murderous act of the anti-moral and diabolical imagination. Frank Rich reports what John Wilkes Booth sings in Stephen Sondheim's *Assassin*, "And all you have to do is move your little finger . . . and you can change the world."[30]

Lincoln told truths that the nation needed to hear and paid for it with his life. The nation lost a vast reservoir of moral imagination to face its most persistent, pernicious, and pervasive moral issues, slavery (institutional racism), race (equality in a multiracial society), and religion (whose religion would dominate the public square). The loss of Lincoln's moral imagination is a tragedy from which the nation has never fully recovered, given that the nation is still fighting over contemporary versions of the same moral issues of slavery, race, and religion. In some sense, we are

---

28. Louis P. Masur, "Lincoln's Final Appeal: The Last Speech of Abraham Lincoln," Historynet, https://www.historynet.com/lincolns-final-appeal-the-last-speech-of-abraham-lincoln.htm.

29. James M. McPherson, *Battle Cry of Freedom: The Civil War Era* (London: Oxford University Press, 1988, 2003), 852.

30. Frank Rich, "Tuesday's Worst Case Scenario," *New York Magazine*, October 29, 2020, https://nymag.com/intelligencer/2020/10/frank-rich-the-2020-elections-worst-case-scenario.html.

fighting the Civil War all over again. The struggle with our greatest human moral dilemma continues: how do individuals, especially in groups—families, clans, factions, political parties, religious persuasions, nations, and states—live together when we are different in religion, culture, politics, interests, and values? How do we overcome the human tendency to violence, hate, oppression, destruction, greed, cruelty, discrimination, domination, war, rape, and pillage in the face of human difference when people move their "little finger" and change the world? My prayer is that we do not surprise ourselves with the levels of violence we can attain.

Chapter 5

WHITE CHRISTIAN NATIONALISM, WHITENESS, AND THE RHETORICAL CONSTRUCTION OF TRIBAL GODS

Most white conservative Christians don't want piety from this president; they want power. In Trump, they see a champion to who will restore them to their rightful place at the center of American life, while using his terrible swift sword to punish their enemies. . . . Christian nationalism is not often really about theology and thus can't be ascribed to all conservative churchgoers. . . . It's about identity, enforcing hierarchy, and order.

—McKay Coppins

I would like to suggest that the vast majority of American political discourse is, in fact, rhetorical and theological. First, given the fact that we live in a "democracy," and the governed must give consent to being governed, the ones who would govern must rhetorically persuade enough voters of the viability of their candidacy or platform. In the effort to persuade, one of the major tools of persuasion is an appeal to God, faith, and religion, both false claims of faith and true belief in God. Also, sometimes religion is an asset and other times a liability to overcome. One only need review the difficulties of the 1960s candidacy of John F. Kennedy as a Catholic running for president and the most recent conspiratorial narratives of Barack Obama being a Muslim during, before, and even after leaving presidential office to understand the complex perceptions about religion that swirl around political office. Beginning with the aforementioned Puritan jeremiads in the 1700s, American political discourse has always had theological appeals, religious undergirding, and divine imperatives. In my estimation, there is a God or an appeal to one connected implicitly or explicitly to most rhetorical discourse in politics.

To illustrate this point of a God connected to American political discourse, I look carefully at former President Donald J. Trump's "performance" of whiteness and its theological worldview and appeal in a representative speech of his rhetoric. Historically, there have been many iterations of white supremacy, but I want to look at its contemporary manifestation by closely and critically examining this phenomenon of white Christian nationalism that provides the spiritual and ideological Christian justification for support of the presidency of Donald J. Trump, particularly from white evangelicals, but also from others in the Roman Catholic church and even some in the Black church. The bottom line is that we can discern from Trump's discourse the rhetorical construction of a tribal god.

The moment I mentioned Trump's performance of whiteness, I interjected race and the ideology of whiteness into our discussion. Trump and the support he has garnered with his racist birtherism and ultimate election ended the pretense of the false illusion during the Obama era of a postracial America. Trump and Trumpism unapologetically and rhetorically centers and privileges whiteness. Trump uses white Christian nationalistic theological claims, among others, to attract and maintain a large part of his audience, and therefore exposes in glaring relief what Kalapana Seshadri-Crooks identifies as the "conceit of whiteness."[1] The word *conceit* carries the connotation of deceit, indicating a personal opinion and overestimation of the judgment of one's character, skills, or abilities. It

---

1. Kalpana Seshadri-Crooks, "The Comedy of Domination: Psychoanalysis and the Conceit of Whiteness," *The Pschoanalysis of Race*, ed. Christopher Lane (New York: Columbia University Press, 1998), 353–79.

is much akin to vanity or pride. Much of this can be found in Trump's rhetoric in his vanity and pride in the white race (the real Americans), and an overestimation of his own personal character, skills, and abilities as a member of said race. This discourse of conceit seeks to rewrite and reinterpret history by discarding unpleasant facts and realities of mistreatment of marginalized people with a fictional and exclusionary mythic narrative of a sublime and idyllic white Christian America—hence white Christian nationalism hearkens back to and seeks to achieve this reality. This mythology fosters the disconnect between the cross and the lynching tree of which we spoke earlier. The way that white Christian nationalism handles the inconvenient truth of white Christian brutality, racism, oppression, and hatred is to delete this unpleasant history from memory and reality. In support of the fictional reality, white Christian nationalism dismisses any viewpoint, protest, truth, perspective, opinion, objection, or dissent that challenges its interpretation of fictional America as un-American, socialist, communist, unpatriotic, anti-white, "playing the race card," divisive, whining, unpatriotic, sometimes using the infamous "America: love it or leave it."

It is important to say that Trump is not the creator nor progenitor of white supremacist ideology. The narrative of whiteness was alive before Trump and will live on well after and without Trump. He is its product, representative, chief opportunist, primary mouthpiece, and faithful servant for this time. I critically examine Trump because he so brazenly and openly practices the ideology of whiteness that he removes all plausible deniability that for generations has attempted to mask white Christian support of racism, sexism, hatred, and bigotry. Donald J. Trump's daily "performance" of white supremacy is intricately connected to and supported by a white Christian theological worldview and appeal. Therefore, my question is: what kind of God are these Christian groups that support Trump serving?

Let me be clear about what I mean when I say white supremacy and whiteness: the privilege of whiteness is assumed and perpetuated across generations so that, taking the historically long view, the majority of property, wealth, and material goods are owned, operated, and institutionalized exclusively for white benefit. In conjunction, whiteness consistently chooses ignorance, innocence, naïveté, blindness, indifference, blame, cultural incompetency, or outright maliciousness, hatred, and violence over the genuine challenge of racial, gender, religious and ethnic equality—material, political, rhetorical, and representational.[2] Allow me to make a few preliminary comments before arriving at my central argument.

I want to stress that Trump's whiteness rhetoric and performance is also about something larger, broader, and deeper in the American psyche than Trump himself. Trump is speaking whiteness, and there is a strong and immoveable audience that fawns, listens, hears, agrees, encourages, and supports his rhetoric and corresponding belligerent actions. There is a sizeable population of adherents who find white Christian nationalistic rhetoric and behavior expressive of their worldview and perspective, and so support it, despite whimsical excuses by some that they wish he would stop tweeting, or "they do not like his personality." This is the argument that suggests that they do not like his character but favor his policies. As if character and policies can be separated. The more Trump's policies are supported, the more it emboldens his questionable character.

In their revealing article on Christian nationalism (which I say more about later), "Make America Christian Again," Whitehead, Perry, and Baker argue that the outcome of the 2020 election would not make a substantial difference to white Christian nationalism. In their concluding statements, they suggest:

> Both before and since the election of Trump, researchers and pundits have hailed the end of "white, Christian America" . . . it is critical to acknowledge that the influence of Christian nationalism can outlive the decline of its progenitors. . . . While white Christians might be declining geographically, one of their primary cultural creations will remain a powerful political force for years, and elections to come.[3]

---

2. Definition borrowed from Thomas Kane, "Bringing the Real: Lacan and Tupac," in *Prospects: An Annual of American Cultural Studies* 27 (2002): 641–63; and Michele Alexander, *The New Jim Crow: Mass Incarceration in the Age of Colorblindness* (New York: New Press, 2010), 203.

3. Andrew L. Whitehead, Samuel L. Perry, and Joseph O. Baker, "Make America Christian Again: Christian Nationalism and Voting for Trump in the 2016 Presidential Election," *Sociology of Religion: A Quarterly Review* 79:2 (2018): 167.

Christian nationalism as a cultural creation of white protestant Christians has been and will remain a powerful political force for years and elections to come. My posture to my children, grandchildren, and all people of goodwill is that we will be dealing with white Christian nationalism for generations. "Eternal vigilance" against it is prudent and necessary, starting with voting as a baseline, and more forms of nonviolent protest.

I am increasingly aware that once race and whiteness are mentioned, we are trapped in the aforementioned global racial paradigm that presents a room with many mirrors from which escape is difficult. We have already discussed that the social construction of race and racism was a post-1400 European construction and invention to justify conquest, pillage, enslavement, and colonialism. Yes, there are other sociocultural hierarchies, such as the caste system and apartheid in other parts of the world that have utilized human difference to broad and systemic effects to demean, manipulate, and control people and resources. But Roger Sanjek suggests that race is a remarkable condensation of social class, cultural practices, and language into physical appearance—specifically skin color, facial features, and hair texture. According to Sanjek, "No other historical or ethnographical order . . . has been as globally inclusive in its assignment of social and cultural difference to 'natural causes' as has post-1400s racism."[4]

The racial paradigm is so overarching and all-encompassing that, as Seshadri-Crooks suggests, we cannot speak of race without becoming invested in it because:

> race organizes difference and elicits investment in its subjects because it promises access to being itself. It offers the prestige of being better and superior; it is the promise of being more human, less lacking. The possibility of enjoyment is at the core of "race."[5]

---

4. Roger Sanjek, "The Enduring Inequalities of Race," in *Race*, 2. Though I basically agree with Sanjek, following Kalpana Seshadri-Crooks, I differ slightly with her claim that the biggest and most devastating historical or ethnographical order has been the patriarchal ordering of "male and female into a binary relationship." Seshadri-Crooks argues, following Lacan, that the binary relationship of male and female is the biggest and most devastating order and race is a close second, that sexual difference escapes or confounds language and produces anxieties that race rhetorically functions to manage. See Kalpana Seshadri-Crooks, *Desiring Whiteness: A Lacanian Analysis of Race* (New York: Routledge, 2000), 7.

5. Seshadri-Crooks, *Desiring Whiteness*, 7.

Racism offers to the racist the prestige of being better and superior, more human and less lacking. And those of us who oppose racism, as Seshadri-Crooks suggests, can become complicit in its paradigm. Even as we oppose the racist paradigm, she argues, "we desire to embrace it."[6] I take her to mean that in critiquing racism and the ideology of whiteness, the temptation is to do what whiteness does, that is, to make oneself superior. In our critique of whiteness, we have the ability to see ourselves as "more human and less lacking."

In this struggle for equality, I have noticed the tendency in myself, a nagging urge when dealing with white supremacy (in its many forms), beneath my angst, anger, and protest to feel morally superior. In my discussion of the performance of whiteness evident in Trump's presidency, and sharply honed in his rhetoric, the temptation is to position myself as a better human being. The effect is to reify the racist system that I stand so deeply against. This is not to suggest that some behaviors are not less moral and, in fact, some actions reveal a character and belief system that is repugnant, less human, and even evil. The challenge is *to be clear about immoral behavior and not use the deficiencies of another to see oneself as "more human and less lacking."*

For example, as many womanists and same-gender loving people historically and currently suggest to much of the African American church, there is hypocrisy in the ability to vehemently critique race and whiteness and yet completely miss the fact that by adopting patriarchy or homophobia the church is operating out of the same "more human, less lacking" paradigm. We all have places where difference must be debilitated, demonized, and dominated for us to feel psychologically secure. The temptation is to look down on others and view oneself as morally superior, more noble, and in essence more human and less lacking. We are forever struggling to become more humane, more comfortable with difference, and more inclusive—all of us in one form or another. Let none of us pretend that the footprint of supremacy is not in our own hearts, though some of us do the work to overcome it.

---

6. Seshadri-Crooks, *Desiring Whiteness*, 7.

The Racial Contract

In *The Racial Contract*, Charles W. Mills uses classic Western social contract theory to take a sweeping look at European expansionism and racism over the last five hundred years. For Mills, a "racial contract" has shaped a system of global European domination establishing relationships between white and nonwhite, accompanied by a system of ideological (including theological) conditioning and force that offers justification and sheer violence if necessary to accomplish its ends.[7] In the American context, the racial contract does not include everyone in democracy in terms of the constitutionally professed language "we the people." Within American democracy, there is a subset of people, the "real people," who categorically count and for whom the benefits, assets, and resources of democracy are meant and intended (including police protection). When we consider Trump's rhetoric, it is clear that when Trump talks about "the people," in the sense of "we the people," he means we the white people and the nonwhites who support him and his agenda. This is not breaking news; marginalized people have always had a birds-eye view of the hypocrisy and venom of white America. Black people, in particular, have lived with, suffered because of, and fully understood in their bodies and psyches the "conceit of whiteness."

Scholars James Golden and Richard Rieke add an interesting perspective when they suggest that racism might be a problem of psychiatry—by which they mean the psyche. They argue that there is something in the psyche of whiteness *"that inhibits the ability of whites to interrogate or engage their most basic beliefs when the speaker is African American."*[8] While W. E. B. DuBois made famous the concept of the "double-consciousness" of African Americans, there is also the "double-consciousness" of whiteness: the consciousness of the stated and professed ideals of democracy and the justification of undemocratic practices operative for the marginalized at any given moment. There is an obvious double standard, and often to make themselves psychologically whole, many whites attempt to disguise

---

7.   Charles W. Mills, *The Racial Contract* (Ithaca, NY: Cornell University Press, 1997).

8.   Joshua Gunn and Mark Lawrence McPhail, "Coming Home to Roost: Jeremiah Wright, Barack Obama and the (re)Signing of (Post) Racial Rhetoric," *Rhetoric Society Quarterly* 45:1 (2015): 6.

it with the innocent and naïve myth of American life as "nonracial." They argue that America is postracial, obvious by the fact that America voted for a Black president—twice. This was one of the factors the Supreme Court used to gut the Voting Rights Act and open the floodgate again for all kinds of tactics of voter suppression to be reengaged. Without digging too deep into Freud, two of my favorite scholars, Joshua Gunn and Mark Lawrence McPhail, connect Freud's theories of jokes to whiteness and suggest:

> The unspeakable joke threatens to expose whiteness as a "ruse" to adopt [Judith] Butler's term. The ruse is that whiteness is only a performance—not the essence—of authority; that as a color whiteness is but one element in a series of difference, and not the inaugural signifier of difference as such; and that whiteness is reducible to a metaphor that is produced in its citation of radical discontinuity—it does not constitute a stable presence.[9]

Many, including myself, have mainly viewed racism as a problem of ignorance and false consciousness, one that can be overcome by moral suasion, "susceptible to persuasion either as rational intervention or as *pietho,* talking cure."[10] Gunn and McPhail challenge the traditional notion of efficacy of persuasion by stating that "racism is not a problem of rational argument, or moral suasion, but the product of deeply held beliefs and values sustained as much by unconscious desire as by rational choice."[11] Racism is a product of a deeply held conscious and unconscious belief publicly performed in the rhetoric and acts of superiority, often with a full measure of faith and religious belief and support. Upon reflection and experience, I have come to believe Gunn and McPhail's premise concerning racism as true—racism is deeply held beliefs and values of superiority sustained as much by unconscious desire as by conscious and rational choice. For a discussion of unconscious choice, please review my chapter

9.   Gunn and McPhail, "Coming Home to Roost," 7.

10.   Gunn and McPhail, "Coming Home to Roost," 7.

11.   Gunn and McPhail, "Coming Home to Roost," 7.

"The Unconscious Moral Worldview and the Dangerous Sermon" in the second book of this trilogy, *Surviving a Dangerous Sermon.*[12]

Trump and Christian Nationalism

There has been much and varied discussion as to the reason(s) for the 2016 election of Trump. There has been much hand-wringing and discussion of polls that were wrong, projections that were inaccurate, and factors that were missed that ended up in the surprising result. Recently, I have been most convinced by the work of several sociologists in a quantitative study that I quoted earlier entitled "Make America Christian Again: Christian Nationalism and Voting for Trump in the 2016 Presidential Election." The authors conclude, based in quantitative data, that "Christian nationalism operates as a set of beliefs and ideals that seek the national preservation of a supposedly unique Christian identity. Voting for Trump was for many Americans a Christian nationalist response to perceived threats to that identity."[13]

The first building block of their argument is to distinguish "civil religion" and "Christian nationalism." Both are closely connected in that they present an exclusive narrative and myth that offers purpose and unity to adherents that they are different and unique. Civil religion is defined as "America's covenantal relationship with a divine creator who promises blessings for the nation fulfilling its responsibilities to defend liberty and justice."[14] Often vaguely connected to Christianity, civil religion rarely refers to Jesus Christ or other explicitly Christian symbols. On the other hand, Christian nationalism is explained as:

> rooted in Old Testament parallels between America and Israel, who was commanded to maintain blood purity, often through war, conquest, and separation. Unlike civil religion, . . . appeals to Christian nationalism are

---

12. Thomas, *Surviving a Dangerous Sermon*, chapter 3: "The Unconscious Moral Worldview and the Dangerous Sermon," 37–59. See also George Lakoff, *Moral Politics: How Liberals and Conservatives Think*, 3rd ed. (Chicago: University of Chicago Press, 2016).

13. Whitehead, Perry, and Baker, "Make America Christian Again," 153.

14. Whitehead, Perry, and Baker, "Make America Christian Again," 150.

often quite explicitly evangelical, and consequently, imply the exclusion
of other religions, faiths or cultures. . . . Christian nationalism is often
linked with racialist sentiments, equating cultural purity with racial or
ethnic exclusion.[15]

What is really interesting beyond these significant clarifications is that,
unlike civil religion, contemporary expressions of Christian nationalism
need not be moored in traditional Christian moral categories and can fea-
ture exclusion, apocalyptic claims, war, and, evidenced in January 2021,
insurrection and overrunning the nation's Capitol in the effort to overturn
democracy.

Many lambast evangelicals for their support of Trump given his obviously questionable moral character and background. Trump is not traditionally religious or recognized (even by supporters) to be of high moral
character. Based in years of being considered the "moral majority," bearers
of "family values," and the judges and critics of the moral character of the
nation and entire groups of people, of course with the backing of God and
interpretations of scripture, the umbrella of Christian nationalism nevertheless allows religious supporters and evangelicals to throw off all of this
earlier moral protestation and support Trump. The result is that:

> the Christian nation myth can function as a symbolic boundary uniting
> both personally religious and irreligious members of conservative groups.
> In this respect, Christian nationalism . . . provides a resilient and malleable
> set of symbols that is not beholden to any particular institution, affiliation
> or moral tradition. This allows its influence to reach beyond the Christian
> tradition of its origins.[16]

The authors also suggest that unmoored Christian nationalism tends toward authoritarian figures and religious indignation (anger and grievance).
The Christian nationalism narrative is very fluid and allows religious and
irreligious members of conservative and extremist far-right groups and
white supremacist militias to, as we would say in the neighborhood that I

---

15. Whitehead, Perry, and Baker, "Make America Christian Again," 150.

16. Whitehead, Perry, and Baker, "Make America Christian Again," 150–51.

grew up in, "get in where they fit in"—Proud Boys, Oath Keepers, Bugaloo Bois, etc.

There is a god imperative in that Trump's direct reference of the Christian nation myth periodically allows various supporters and endorsers to make the connection between voting for Trump and the United States as a Christian nation. The authors concluded that—longing and pining for the myth of America's distinctly Christian past, nervous and insecure about a Christian future based on no longer being the majority in America, and further fermented in Trump's apocalyptic campaign rhetoric—"Americans adhering to Christian nationalist ideology were more likely to vote for Trump."[17] They suggest that Christian nationalism operates as a set of beliefs and ideals that seek the national preservation of a unique Christian identity. A vote for Trump was a vote against this perceived threat to that identity. They concluded that, even accounting for factors such as economic dissatisfaction, sexism, racism, Islamaphobia, and xenophobia, "a vote for Trump was a symbolic defense of the United States's perceived Christian heritage"[18]—adherence to a Christian nationalistic identity and ideology.

Trump made obvious appeals to Christian nationalist sentiment by repeating the refrain that United States is abdicating its Christian heritage. The authors make the very interesting point that I completely missed. They argue that the media again focused on whether the Religious Right would support a nonpious candidate and from various quarters called it hypocrisy. At Liberty University on January 18, 2016, Trump quoted a Bible verse as being from "two Corinthians," rather than the usual "Second Corinthians." Media and many preachers I know focused on whether or not the lack of knowledge about the Bible would affect religious voters; they totally overlooked the next words out of his mouth, which were a direct appeal to Christian nationalism:

> But we are going to protect Christianity. And if you look what's going on throughout the world, you look at Syria where they're, if you're Christian, they're chopping off heads. You look at the difference places, and Christianity,

---

17. Whitehead, Perry, and Baker, "Make America Christian Again," 152.

18. Whitehead, Perry, and Baker, "Make America Christian Again," 152.

it's under siege. I'm a Protestant. I'm very proud of it. Presbyterian to be exact. But I'm very proud of it, very, very proud of it. And we've gotta protect, because bad things are happening, very bad things are happening, and we don't—I don't know what it is—we don't band together, maybe. Other religions, frankly, they're banding together and they're using it. And here we have, if you look at this country, it's gotta be 70 percent, 75 percent, some people say even more, the power we have, somehow we have to unify. We have to band together. . . . Our country has to do that around Christianity (applause).[19]

This appeal is exactly what I mean when I say that political discourse is rhetorical and theological. There is a god imperative in Trump's direct reference of the Christian nation myth. This myth allows various supporters and endorsers to make the connection between voting for Trump and the United States as a Christian nation, in the face of their no longer being the majority and therefore their lack of interest in racial equality.

Ironically, Christian nationalism is focused on preserving a perceived Christian identity for America irrespective of the means by which such a project would be achieved, going against stated moral beliefs, constitutional mandates, and norms of democracy—for instance, packing the judiciary, including the Supreme Court; voter suppression; and seeking to overturn legitimate elections with illicit claims of voter fraud. Whitehead, Perry, and Baker suggest that "Christian nationalistic rhetoric can used effectively by almost anyone promising to defend American's 'Christian heritage,' even a thrice married, nonpious, self-proclaimed public playboy."[20]

Projections of the end of white Christian America are premature. While there are demographic shifts that ensure that white Protestants will not be the demographic majority and will decline in cultural hegemony, Christian nationalism will outlive this decline. The large tent of Christian nationalism created by white Protestants will be a political, economic, and social force to be contended with well beyond what the demographics bely. I advocate eternal vigilance against the god of Christian nationalism.

19. C-Span, "Presidential Candidate Donald Trump at Liberty University," video posted by C-Span, January 18, 2016, https://www.c-span.org/video/?403331-1/donald-trump-remarks-liberty-university.

20. Whitehead, Perry, and Baker, "Make America Christian Again," 166.

That god was certainly evoked in Trump's public "performance of whiteness" and Christian nationalism in the June 1, 2020, Rose Garden Speech and photo-op at St. John's Episcopal Church.

Trump's "Performance of Whiteness"

To carefully look at Trump's public performance of whiteness in the Rose Garden Speech and at St. John's Church, we must briefly engage critical tools of rhetorical criticism. Aristotle's classic definition of rhetoric is "the ability to discover the available means of persuasion." Rhetorical criticism is the study of the various persuasive options available to speakers in the creation of speech texts and how those options work together to create effects in the speaker and audience. Rhetorical criticism allows us to see with greater clarity both the persuasive choices the speaker made and potentially other choices that were not selected. One methodology within the field of rhetorical criticism is that of close reading, which I utilize to examine Trump's attempt to persuade in the Rose Garden speech and photo-op at St. John's Church. First, let me briefly explain first, second, and third persona.

First, Second, and Third Persona of Rhetorical Criticism

From the overarching perspective of how a speaker persuades an audience, every speaker adopts a persona. For Aristotle, every orator had three modes of proof that make persuasion possible—ethos, pathos, and logos. *Logos* is the logical thought structure of the speech, *pathos* is the emotion, conviction, or passion that a speaker brings to the oratorical moment, and, what Aristotle said is the most important of the proofs, *ethos* is the character, the credibility of the speaker with the audience in regards to the subject matter at hand. The reason that we listen to, for example, Warren Buffett so intently when he speaks about investments is that his successful investing track record gives him a large cache of credibility.

As part of establishing ethos or credibility, all speakers develop a "persona." Persona is a role or identity a speaker constructs and adopts to convey ethos or credibility as part of the strategy of persuasion. Historically, the term *persona* is derived from theater, the wearing of a mask to play a part. In the best sense of the meaning of the word, and not in the sense of necessarily being false, persona is the mask that the speaker brings to the platform, the appearance one presents to the world in the oratorical moment. Persona is not only the spoken word that the speaker constructs, but ultimately the total package of how the speaker engages the rhetorical moment and speech, including clothing and dress, social media posts and profile, props, appointments and symbols, decorations and settings, and attention to place. Rhetorical critical scholars have labeled this intended and projected persona by the speaker, the "first persona." It is the total orchestrated and desired effect of words, symbols, setting, and occasion created and intended by the speaker to convey meaning to an audience.

A close reading of the Rose Garden address and subsequent trip to St. John's church reveals that Trump crafts first persona as a "strongman persona," what he calls a "law and order president" to appeal to and persuade his voting base through the values and tenets of white Christian nationalism.

In his groundbreaking article, "Second Persona," Edwin Black argues that every discourse has a first persona and also a "second persona," an audience that the speech is targeted to persuade. The second persona, or the targeted audience, can be discerned based upon the moral tint of ideology in the speech. Black argues that a speaker cannot help but cast a moral shadow from the first persona upon the audience. The metaphors and images the speaker uses are the tips of "ideology" in the discourse. Metaphors are not accidental, but are purposefully intentional and expressive of the character of the first persona and are intended to persuade the audience shaped in the mind of the speaker. For Black, ideology in the discourse wants the audience to be something. We make the discourse moral or immoral by accepting or rejecting what the speaker in the discourse asks us to be. The rhetorical critic can discern the moral character of both speaker and audience based upon acceptance or rejection of the speaker's persuasive attempt.[21]

Philip Wander, arguing that identification of second persona is important in a world of differing ideologies, built upon Black's second persona to create "the third persona" that is not invited into the conversation. The third persona is the audience that is negated or rejected, sometimes intentionally and sometimes outside the awareness or cognizance of the speaker and speech. Wander states:

> [J]ust as the discourse may be understood to affirm certain characteristics, it may also be understood to imply other characteristics, roles, actions, or ways of seeing things to be avoided. What is negated through the Second Persona forms the silhouette of a Third Persona—the "it" that is not present, that is objectified in a way that "you" and "I" are not.[22]

While the metaphors of the speaker (first persona) target the audience (second persona) to be and become, the "it" (third persona) is the summation of all that the audience (second persona) are told to avoid becoming. The third persona through the speech is being negated in history, a being whose presence is silenced through presentation as the exact opposite of the speaker's moral ideal. It is present in this speech by Trump, this third persona, who, based upon the speaker's rhetoric and action, cannot assemble nor protest.

Based upon the fact that people in third persona are not fairly represented and are often lied about and caricatured as evil and demonic, they are not allowed to speak for themselves and, as a result, are suppressed and oppressed rhetorically, as they are in physical reality. In most cases, the third persona refers to groups who have been historically denied citizenship and human rights and considered "other" or, in Trump's case, not "real" Americans. Third persona can be assigned by the speaker based on age, country, gender, sexual preference, race, religion, or other parameters. These individuals or groups are objectified, disinherited, and dispossessed,

---

21. Edwin Black, "The Second Persona," *The Quarterly Journal of Speech* 56:2 (April 1970).

22. Philip Wander, "The Third Persona: An Idealogical Turn in Rhetorical Theory," *Central States Speech Journal* 34:1 (1984): 312.

and their moral positions are not worthy of consideration. They are silenced by the discourse.

I examine Trump's Rose Garden speech and march to St. John's Episcopal Church from the perspective of an audience member who is in the position of third persona, a person who protests the treatment of African American citizens at the hands of systemic and institutionalized police violence.

The Rose Garden Speech and St. John's Church

On June 1, 2020, Trump gave what some have called his "Anti-Riot Speech" from the Rose Garden at the White House. The background was more than a hundred thousand deaths registered from the once-in-a-century health pandemic COVID-19 and many American cities filled with a generational movement of protesters not seen since the civil rights movement, who were decrying yet another example of police violence against African Americans in the death of George Floyd. The overall message of the speech was for Trump to continue to brand himself as the "law and order president."

The term "law and order" has controversial baggage as a powerful political trope from the late 1960s, made popular by then governor Ronald Reagan and presidential candidate Richard Nixon. Nixon as a part of his election strategy appealed to working-class white ethnics in northern cities to vote against the Democratic Party based on the argument that Democrats were "soft on crime" and not willing to punish rioters with the law to maintain order. Conservatives like Nixon and Reagan argued that the role of the national government was to promote respect and protection for personal security and private property. Those who riot, loot, and commit arson or other forms of "violence" violate "law and order" and should be prosecuted regardless of justifications of cause such as racial grievance. In adopting the persona of the "law and order" president, Trump remixes and adopts Nixon and Reagan–era conservative arguments and justifications that would be familiar to his principle base, white nationalist conservatives. The negative meaning was very clear to protesters and Trump supporters: law and order will crush protests and protesters.

Trump opens the speech by stating to his "fellow Americans," that his highest duty is to defend "our great country and the American people."[23] He announces that he swore to uphold the laws of the nation and that is exactly what he intends to do. He then speaks to the death of George Floyd and the subsequent protests:

> All Americans were rightly sickened and revolted by the brutal death of George Floyd. My administration is fully committed that for George and his family, justice will be served. He will not have died in vain. But we cannot allow the righteous cries and peaceful protesters to be drowned out by an angry mob. The biggest victims of the rioting are peace-loving citizens in our poorest communities. And as their president, I will fight to keep them safe. I will fight to protect you. I am your president of law and order, and an ally of all peaceful protesters.

Trump initially appears to be rhetorically supportive and an ally of peaceful protesters of the death of George Floyd. While claiming to support peaceful protesters, their supporters, and peace-loving citizens of these communities, in actuality he positions them in the third persona:

> But in recent days, our nation has been gripped by professional anarchists, violent mobs, arsonists, looters, criminals, rioters, Antifa, and others. These are not acts of peaceful protest. These are acts of domestic terror. The destruction of innocent life and the spilling of innocent blood is an offense to humanity and a crime against God.

Trump uses the metaphors of *professional anarchists, violent mobs, arsonists, looters, and criminals,* and then assigns the source of the violence to Antifa. In a balanced and fair report entitled "What is Antifa? Is it a group or an idea, and what do supporters want?" CBS News sets forth several salient points to help readers understand the true nature of Antifa.

> The term "Antifa" is short for anti-fascist. . . . In general, people who identify as Antifa are known not for what they *support*, but what they *oppose*: Fascism, nationalism, far-right ideologies, white supremacy, authoritarianism,

---

23. All references to the speech are from this transcript: "President Donald Trump's June 1 Anti-Riot Speech, June 1, 2020," Newsmax, https://www.newsmax.com/politics/riot-anarchists-white-house-speech/2020/06/01/id/970052/.

racism, homophobia and xenophobia. Some Antifa activists also denounce capitalism and the government overall. Antifa actions have included everything from tracking and publicly identifying members of alt-right groups to physically *attacking* adversaries.[24]

There is much more, but this will give the reader at least some of the balanced sense of Antifa. After arson and looting broke out amid the George Floyd protests in Minneapolis, FBI Director Christopher Wray said,

> We're seeing people who are exploiting this situation to pursue violent, extremist agendas—anarchists like ANTIFA, and other agitators. These individuals have set out to sow discord and upheaval, rather than join in the righteous pursuit of equality and justice.[25]

Trump's condemnation of Antifa is not at issue because many Democrats, including Joe Biden and many others, also condemn Antifa. It is his insistent refusal to put the same critique and condemnation on white supremacist organizations, despite the evidence from numerous reports that far-right groups are much more likely involved in violence as "professional anarchists, violent mobs, arsonists, looters, criminals, and rioters."[26] Specific to the George Floyd protesters to which Trump referred, CNN reported that militias and other nonstate actors, right and left, also actively and assertively intervened in the demonstrations, not just Antifa:

> Nonstate actors engaged in more than 100 demonstrations, mostly in response to Black Lives Matter protests, the report states. Those actors include militias and groups from the right and left, such as Antifa, the Proud Boys, the Boogaloo Bois and the Ku Klux Klan.[27]

It is Trump's refusal to condemn violence on both sides, left and right, that is objectionable. Not only in this speech, but in much of his recurring

---

24. Leslie Gorenstein, "What is Antifa? Is it a group or an idea, and what do supporters want?" CBS News, October 16, 2020, https://www.cbsnews.com/news/what-is-antifa/.

25. Gorenstein, "What is Antifa?"

26. Jenny Gross, "Far-Right Groups Are Behind Most U.S. Terrorist Attacks," *The New York Times*, October 25, 2020, https://news.yahoo.com/far-groups-behind-most-u-150611907.html.

27. Harmeet Kaur, "About 93% of Racial Justice Protests in the US Have Been Peaceful," CNN, September 4, 2020, https://www.cnn.com/2020/09/04/us/blm-protests-peaceful-report-trnd/index.html.

rhetoric, Trump finds it difficult to condemn the Proud Boys, the Booga-loo Bois, the Ku Klux Klan (far right extremists and white supremacists) because, for him, they are part of the second persona, his targeted audience and base. He does not want to lose their support so he only condemns Antifa.

Trump heightens the drama of Antifa by calling it "domestic terror," and equates it to the understandings of international terrorism against the United States. He makes moral claims against Antifa equivalent with the violence of international terrorism, raising his language to the language against international terrorism—the "shedding of innocent blood" and "an offense to humanity and a crime against God."[28] Again, far right-wing groups and militias get no such condemnation, and this is "red meat" to his conservative base. It combines the familiar and historical rhetoric of the white backlash of Nixon and Reagan of law and order to the Bush-coined "war on terror" following the terrorist attacks of 9-11-01. As their (protesters') law and order president, with all of the historical baggage that was earlier described in the use of the phrase, Trump grossly exaggerates the threat and source of the violence in order to stoke racial fear in his white audience and white Christian nationalist base.

Trump then announces that "America needs creation not destruction, cooperation not contempt, security not anarchy, healing not hatred, justice not chaos." He declares this as "our mission and we will succeed 100%. Our country always wins." He implies that terrorists like Antifa are not of "our country," like international terrorists, and declares, "we always win." Again, if he denounced all domestic terrorists, left and right, he would appeal to all Americans, make the country safer for all, and we all would win. Instead, he announces that he is taking immediate presidential action to "restore safety and security in America," in effect *for his base*. He will stop the looting, rioting, and arson, and "restore safety and security in America." He will protect the rights of law-abiding Americans. He gives himself completely away as to his true audience, his base, when he adds

---

28.   During the summer of 2019, Republican Senators Ted Cruz and Bill Cassidy introduced a resolution calling for Antifa to be categorized as a domestic terror organization, with Trump voicing his support across Twitter: "Major consideration is being given to naming ANTIFA an 'ORGANIZATION OF TERROR.' Portland is being watched very closely," Donald J. Trump, @realDonaldTrump, Twitter, August 17, 2019.

"including your *second amendment rights*." The mention of taking away second amendment rights is a right-wing talking point that generates tremendous anger and animosity. This is another metaphor indicative of who the second persona is—his base that fears the government is coming to take their guns. If a city or state refuses to take action, he will deploy the "United States military and quickly solve the problem for them." He pledges to protect the "great Capitol," Washington, DC, with "armed soldiers, military personnel, and law enforcement." Those who threaten innocent life and property will be arrested and prosecuted to the full extent of the law and he includes "Antifa and others who are leading instigators of this violence." He will not include white supremacist terrorists in his prohibition. He says, "One law and order that is what it is." Once it is restored, "we will help you, we will help your business, and we will help your family." Out of his law and order appeal, he again reemphasizes the law:

> America is founded upon the rule of law. It is the foundation of our prosperity, our freedom and our very way of life. But where there is no law, there is no opportunity. Where there is no justice, there is no liberty. Where there is no safety, there is no future. We must never give in to anger or hatred. If malice or violence reigns, then none of us is free.

He then closes the speech by expressing his "true and passionate love for our country" and saying, "The country's greatest days are ahead." He says, "Thank you very much," and announces that he is "going to pay his respects to a very, very special place." Trump and his entourage then proceed to St. John's Episcopal Church.

Though Trump speaks of supporting protesters in the Rose Garden, at the very moment of the speech, law enforcement officers used tear gas and rubber bullets to disperse peaceful and law-abiding protesters and forcibly remove them from Lafayette Square and surrounding streets to create a path for Trump and senior administration officials to walk from the White House to St John's Church. The violence of this physical removal is even more proof of my assertion that peaceful protesters and their supporters are the third persona of this speech. St. John's Church had been damaged during protests by fire the night before. Trump walks up to St John's Church, stands there for pictures, and eventually holds a Bible upside down. When asked by a reporter if the Bible was his, Trump responds, "It's a Bible." Trump poses for more photos, brings in part of his team for several other photos, and then says, "America is the greatest country in the world." Leaving the scene, he remarks that he's going to "keep it [America] nice and safe." Trump and entourage process back to the White House.

Trump's Rose Garden speech and jaunt to St. John's Church is designed to appeal to his white Christian nationalist base, both religious and irreligious conservative whites nervous about violence, looting, risk of personal security, and protection of private property. It is a direct appeal to white conservative Christian evangelicals, Roman Catholics, and other religious groups that helped Trump win the 2016 election. The speech, as well as utilization of St. John's Church and the Bible as props, are specifically designed to unite his base around a law-and-order Christian nationalist agenda.

For all intents and purposes, I would suggest that Trump persuades significant parts of his white Christian nationalist base. The speech and especially the jaunt to St. John's Church was covered live by many cable news stations and instantly decried by Democrats as an unbecoming photo-op. In contradistinction to this view of the speech and visit to St. John's Church, Elizabeth Dias writes:

> But in Sioux Center, many evangelicals once again received a different message. . . . "To me it was like, that's great. Trump is recognizing the Bible, we are one nation under God," Mr. Schouten said. "He is willing to stand out there and take a picture of it for the country to see." He added: "Trump was standing up for Christianity."[29]

McKay Coppin, writer for *The Atlantic,* spoke on the phone the night of June 1, 2020, with Dallas megachurch pastor and unfaltering Trump ally Robert Jeffress, and he sounded almost gleeful. Jeffress said, "I thought

29.   Elizabeth Dias, "Christianity Will Have Power," *The New York Times,* November 1, 2020, https://www.nytimes.com/2020/08/09/us/evangelicals-trump-christianity.html?referringSource=article Share.

it was *completely* appropriate for the president to stand in front of that church, . . . And by holding up the Bible, he was showing us that it teaches that, yes, God hates racism, it's despicable—but God also hates lawlessness. . . . I'm happy."[30] Coppin says that all through the night following the trip to St. John's Church, evangelicals cheered Trump's performance on Twitter.

Trump and the collection of speechwriters, handlers, arrangers, and orchestraters of the Rose Garden speech and visit to St. John's Episcopal Church on June 1, 2020, are collectively the first persona. The second persona is Trump's voting base, the collective of white Christian nationalists who support, affirm, and endorse his presidency. Andrew L. Whitehead, one of the authors of "Make America Christian Again," found that:

> white Protestants who believe most strongly that Christianity should hold a privileged place in America's public square are more likely than others to agree with statements such as "We must crack down on troublemakers to save our moral standards and keep law and order" and "Police officers shoot blacks more often because they are more violent than whites."[31]

This is the principal group that forms the second persona.

The third persona can be identified as the sum total of anyone protesting systemic racism and police violence against Black people that led to the death of George Floyd, whether they physically protest or not. Trump and speechwriters crafted the speech and episode at St. John's Episcopal Church to persuade the white Christian nationalist base and exclude people of the third persona.

White Christian nationalism seeks to rewrite and reinterpret history by discarding unpleasant facts and realities of mistreatment of marginalized people with a fictional and exclusionary mythic narrative of a sublime and idyllic white Christian America. The goal of white Christian nationalism is to return to and maintain this fictional reality, dismissing any viewpoint, protest, or dissent that challenges that interpretation of America.

---

30.   McKay Coppin, "The Christians Who Loved Trump's Stunt," *The Atlantic,* June 2, 2020, https://www.theatlantic.com/politics/archive/2020/06/trumps-biblical-spectacle-outside-st-johns-church/612529/.

31.   Coppin, "The Christians Who Loved Trump's Stunt."

The white Christian nationalism myth seeks to make into the third persona anyone who does not support the myth. One person whom white supremacy made third persona is Jeremiah A. Wright Jr. when he told truth that white America did not want to hear.[32] Tim Wise writes that white America's unquestioned investment in the portrait of an idealized America is "so divorced from the reality of the times in which they were produced, as to raise serious questions about the sanity of those who found them so moving, so accurate, so real." Wise lambasts America's so-called "good old days," juxtaposing *Father Knows Best* with Strom Thurman's filibuster speech killing civil rights legislation, and *Leave It to Beaver* with Arkansas Governor Orville Faubus's use of armed force to block black students from entering Little Rock high school. "*That* was America of the 1950s: a brutal, racist reality for millions, not the sanitized version into which so many escape thanks to the miracle of syndication, which merely allows . . . people to live a lie, year after year after year."[33]

It is obvious that this idyllic Christian America is, as is all history in some form, a socially constructed narrative, most often written by "the winners." It would seem natural that if one socially constructs a history, one socially constructs a God to go with that history, hence the invention of tribal gods.

Rhetorical theology discerns our moral imagination and theology through our observable behavior in the world, especially to those who are not of our tribe or our group. If our behavior in the world is racist, hateful, and oppressive, then it follows that the god of our moral imagination is racist, hateful, and oppressive, and, despite what we proclaim in our theology, we are, in fact, serving a tribal god. The tribal god is the god of cultural purity, racial and ethnic exclusion, racist tropes, demonization of opponents, apocalyptic claims, authoritarianism, and religious indignation. In our explication of rhetorical theology, we explore the God persona of our rhetoric.

---

32. For more info on Jeremiah A. Wright Jr., see Frank A. Thomas, "Prophetic Transformation: Jeremiah A. Wright Jr. and the American Dream," in *American Dream 2.0: A Christian Way Out of the Great Recession* (Nashville: Abingdon Press, 2012).

33. Tim Wise, "Of National Lies and Racial Amnesia: Jeremiah Wright, Barack Obama, and the Audacity of Truth," blog, March 18, 2008, http://www.timwise.org/2008/03/of-national-lies-and-racial-amnesia-jeremiah-wright-barack-obama-and-the-audacity-of-truth/.

Finally, based upon Trump's blatant appeal to white Christian nationalism, it is fair to specifically ask, from his metaphors in the ideology and rhetoric of the Rose Garden speech and visit to St. John's Episcopal Church, what does Trump want the audience to be? Remember, from our discussion of the second persona, the moral character of both speaker and audience can be discerned based upon what the speaker invites the audience to be and those who consent to or reject said invitation. Trump is asking the audience to participate in cultural purity, racial and ethnic exclusion, racist tropes, demonization of opponents, apocalyptic claims, authoritarianism, white grievance, and religious indignation. Trump is rhetorically constructing a tribal god and asking the audience to serve this god.

Section Three

THE GOD OF THE DANGEROUS SERMON

THE GOD OF THE DANGEROUS SERMON

One wonders why Christians today get off so easily. Is it because unchristian Americans are that much better than unchristian Romans, or is our light so dim that the tormentor can't see it? What are the things we do that are worth persecuting?

—Clarence Jordan

In light of our critical question "Why have some so much and others so little?" in this final chapter I lay out critical points of the theological side of rhetorical theology.

First, I briefly recap my working gospel of the "Prophetic Messiah" in order to clearly demonstrate Jesus's adherence to a universal rather than a tribal God.[1] It is commonly assumed in many theological circles that Jesus's universal God is not fully revealed until the coming of Pentecost in Acts 2 and Peter's actions at Cornelius's house in Acts 10. My argument is that the universal God of the Dangerous Sermon is revealed in Jesus's inaugural sermon in his hometown of Nazareth. Jesus makes God known as one who is inclined to the poor, oppressed, and captive and stands outside of human perceptions of favoritism, hate, privilege, wealth, and supremacy.

Second, while a tribal god leads to and condones violence, intimidation, theft, and assault, real and rhetorical, we see in Luke 4 that the

---

1. See Thomas, *Surviving a Dangerous Sermon,* "The Prophetic Messiah," 23–52.

universal God of the Dangerous Sermon presents judgment and healing to the entire human community. I explore practical and tangible human behaviors that the universal God would condone or not condone.

Third, I specifically discuss several theological questions that were raised and linger from previous chapters in the struggle for racial equality, such as Frederick Douglass's concern with Lincoln's Second Inaugural that too much forgiveness leads to too much acceptance. In other words, what is the relationship between forgiveness and accountability?

Fourth, at the end of the Lincoln chapter, I quoted Stephen Sondheim from his play *Assassins*, where he raises the question of changing the world by pulling a trigger on a gun with one's "little finger." Is there an alternative to the claim of power to change the world because one has a gun and uses one's "little finger"? Will racial equality, or any movement for justice and liberation for that matter, be continually stifled by those who use their "little finger"?

Finally, are there any possibilities of moral imagination outside of the global racial paradigm? Henceforth, will humanity always be trapped in the 1400s global racial paradigm or are there other possibilities? I want to discuss the reality and role of the church led by the Spirit of God presenting a vision of a new humanity outside the racial paradigm. Let's begin with the prophetic messiah who proclaims a universal God.

The Prophetic Messiah

Mark, Matthew, and Luke all tell of an episode in Jesus's hometown in which his sermon is rejected by his familial neighbors (Matthew 13:54-58, Luke 4:14-30, and Mark 6:1-6a). Luke's purpose is to establish Jesus's inaugural sermon as the programmatic cornerstone of his ministry. The text in Luke opens in verse 4:14 (ASV) by mentioning that Jesus, "in the power of the Spirit," returns to Galilee. Eventually, he comes home to Nazareth, to his family, friends, and the community that raised him. The Lukan text in verse 16 says that he goes to synagogue, as is his custom. He is given the scroll of the prophet Isaiah. Jesus unrolls the scroll, finds Isaiah 61:1-2 (NRSV), and reads:

> The Spirit of the Lord God is upon me, because the Lord has anointed me
> to bring good news to the poor. He has sent me to proclaim release to the
> captives and recovery of sight to the blind, and to let the oppressed go free,
> to proclaim the year of the Lord's favor.

Jesus rolls up the scroll, gives it back to the attendant, and sits down. The
congregation would have seen that as a sign for the beginning of a teaching, an interpretation of the text just presented, and therefore, their eyes
were fixed upon him. Jesus declares in Luke 4:21 (NRSV): "Today, this
scripture has been fulfilled in your hearing." The congregation is amazed.

Jesus declared himself the fulfillment of the prophetic scripture, the
Messiah, the long-awaited one for the deliverance of Israel. What until
now had been potential, promise, and hope for the arrival of the Messiah
is a present reality and is fulfilled. The Messiah has come. But what did
this declaration of the coming of the Messiah mean? What kind of messiah is Jesus?

One scholar convincingly argues that by quoting Isaiah, Jesus builds
on the imagery of the Jubilee year mandated in Leviticus 25:23-55. Every
fifty years, Israel was to declare a "year of liberty," based upon God's prior
action of liberation in freeing them from slavery and hard labor in Egypt.
Practically, the Jubilee laws would have prevented the accumulation of
wealth, particularly capital in the form of land, in any one single family's
hands. Rather, once in a lifetime, the entire economy would be given
a fresh start. History gives no evidence that a Jubilee year was ever celebrated. Such disruption was very difficult, if not impossible, based upon
human political, economic, and social upheaval to protected interests. But
from Jesus's perspective, this is exactly the point. Jubilee is only possible by
the proclamation of the in-breaking reign of God. The year of Jubilee proclaimed by Jesus represented a titanic shift in allegiance from loyalties to
the temporal human order to a new participation in God's reign of justice
and peace. God has good news for the poor, a future of healing and release
from various and all forms of captivity. In Jesus's presence and preaching
of the year of Jubilee, the new order of promise has taken on human flesh
and has been fulfilled "today."

131

In this Lukan version, the hometown audience asks, "Is this Joseph's son?" The exact tone of their question is difficult to interpret. What is clear is how Jesus interpreted their comments. He says to them: "Undoubtedly, you will quote this saying to me: 'Doctor, heal thyself'" (Luke 4:23), and "no prophet is welcome in the prophet's hometown" (Luke 4:24). He makes clear that the meaning of the declaration of the text has been fulfilled; he does not pacify them. He challenges them in the full expansiveness of the reign of God based in the fact that the "year of the Lord's favor" would not be quite what they expected.

Jesus then refers to Elijah's healing of the widow of Zarepath and Elisha's healing of Naaman (1 Kings 17:8-9 and 2 Kings 5:14, respectively). These prophets perform their healing acts among Gentiles and not exclusively for Israelites alone. The healing work of Elijah and Elisha did touch Israel, but it began outside the Jewish community. Sharon Ringe suggests:

> Luke 4:25–27 portrays Jesus telling the townspeople that their longing for evidence of the fulfillment of which he spoke might well not come to them first of all. They have no priority of place, and, as John had warned earlier (3:8), no basis on which to claim privilege in this divine project.[2]

The wrath of the hometown family, friends, and relatives exploded. They drove him to the hill so as to represent ridding the city of defilement, as if he were a plague or were speaking of the blasphemous worship of a foreign god. We would know them, in their response, as a lynch mob. It was a dangerous sermon, and they wanted to kill him for it. Jewish hearers believed that they had the inside track, but in Jesus's sermon, the presumption that salvation is the exclusive right of Jews is revoked. The *New Pillar Commentary* suggests: "By identifying Gentiles as models of faith in a sermon to Jews, Jesus made the revolutionary point that salvation is not limited for Jews, but also includes Gentiles. The sermon in Nazareth effectively anchors the Gentile mission, not in

---

2. Sharon H. Ringe, *Luke* (Louisville: John Knox, 1995), 69.

the later conversion of Cornelius (Acts 10), as often supposed, but in the initial proclamation of the gospel by Jesus himself."[3]

Luke is suggesting that the extension of the gospel to Gentiles in Acts 10 was not an afterthought because Jews rejected Jesus. It was the result of divine election of Gentiles, already operative in the days of Elijah and Elisha and, indeed, even in the days of Abraham, who at the time was called a Gentile (Genesis 11–12). They could not hear this painful truth: that if they did not affirm salvation for the Gentiles, then they could not affirm it for themselves. In this atmosphere of anger, rage, hostility, and venom at the edge of a cliff, the text of Luke 4:30 says that Jesus walks right through the crowd and goes his way. Luke is clear that Jesus's agenda, mission, and work are established despite protestations in service to a tribal God. Jesus is the prophetic messiah and Jesus's God is a universal God. The God Jesus proclaims breaks down human barriers and includes others who are not of our preferred group. While many think the inclusive vision of the church begins in Acts, I believe that it is at the very heart of Jesus's ministry, given that he announces to his hometown a universal God, the God of the Dangerous Sermon.

I am not sure we capture the deep and profound emotions of outrage by Jesus's hometown neighbors in this text. Clarence Jordan in his *Cotton Patch* series thought it was important to translate not only the words, but also the context. Jordan offers a fresh Cotton Patch version of what happened after Jesus proclaims the scripture has been fulfilled in their hearing (italics are mine):

> Then he [Jesus] continued, "Surely some of you will cite to me the old proverb, 'Doctor take your own medicine. Let us see you do right here in your own hometown all the things we heard you did in Columbus [Georgia].'" Well, tell the truth, no prophet is welcome in his own hometown. And I'm telling you straight, there were a lot of *white* widows in Georgia during the time of Elijah, when the skies were locked up for three years and six months, and there was a great drought everywhere, but Elijah didn't stay with any of them. Instead, he stayed with a *Negro* woman over in Terrill County

3. James R. Edwards, *The New Pillar Commentary: The Gospel According to Luke* (Grand Rapids: Eerdman, 2015), 132–33.

[Georgia]. And there were a lot of sick *white* people during the time of the great preacher Elisha, but he didn't heal any of them—only Namaan, the African. When they heard that, the whole congregation blew a gasket. They jumped up, ran him out of the town, and dragged him to the top of the hill on which the city was built, with the intention of pushing him off. But he got up and walked right through the middle of the whole mob and went his way.[4]

This captures the racial tension and sense of outrage of the text in the contemporary emotional truth of segregated Georgia in the 1960s in a manner very similar to those of Jesus's day.

The God Who Touches the Goodness of People

Not only does rhetorical theology deconstruct tribal gods, it also constructs a universal and inclusive God. The God of the Dangerous Sermon, based in the preacher's moral imagination:

- helps adherents to see the humanity of people who are different, particularly not of one's group, and to display the positive attributes of empathy and compassion;

- will not participate in or support individual or institutional racism, misogyny, homophobia, hate, violence, stereotypes, conspiracy theories, mob violence, and the oppression and demonization of people, especially the poor, for any reason, justification, or rationale;

- will not allow suspension of stated theological moral principles for any reason. One of the classic tactics that allows people to demonize others is to rhetorically build the case that the behavior of the other is so evil, vile, and despicable that moral values must be suspended to defeat the enemy, including killing, murder, maiming, lynching, etc. The God of the Dangerous Sermon proclaims that our moral principles are not contingent upon the behavior of other people and can never justify killing, murder, maiming, lynching, etc.;

---

4. Jordan, *Cotton Patch Gospel: Luke and Acts*, Luke 4:23-30.

134

- is a universal God who judges both individuals and nations based upon a clear distinction between God's purposes and the often partial purposes of human beings. God's purposes are above, beyond, and often mysterious to the designs of any human being, flag, party, nation, form of nationalism, family, or group. The question is not if the God of the Dangerous Sermon is on our side, but are we on the side of the God of the Dangerous Sermon?

- will offer forgiveness and favor as well as judgment and penalty. If our God only offers forgiveness and favor and never judgement and penalty, this is not the universal God. There are boundaries and limits to the compassion of God, who punished Israel and, according to Lincoln, punished America for the sin of slavery. Also, as Lincoln and the Hebrew Bible suggested, beyond punishment there is grace;

- does not condone divine claims of the stealing of land, resources, people, or wealth in any institutional and individual form;

- does not offer divine guarantees that all earthly enemies will be destroyed and any group will be given dominance generation upon generation;

- is not the god of our privilege such that any affront to our privilege is an affront to the human race and Godself;

- a God active in orchestrating human events toward God's mysterious ends.

Theology declares our God and rhetoric reveals our God at the level of ethical behavior, particularly in regards to those not of our group or clan.

In my earlier book, *How to Preach a Dangerous Sermon,* I referenced Ruby Sales's argument that there is a spiritual crisis in white America, specifically, a crisis of meaning. In regard to that crisis, and in my words, proclaiming the God of the Dangerous Sermon, Sales asks, "How do we raise people up from disposability to essentiality?" and further:

> [Sales] asks what is the public theology that can say to the white person in Massachusetts or the forty-five-year-old person in Appalachia, who is heroin addicted because they feel their lives have no meaning, often the

result of the trickle-down whiteness in the world today, that their lives matter? She argues that many white people have been told their whole lives that their essence is whiteness, power, and domination, and when that no longer exists, they feel like they are dying or get caught up in the throes of death.[5]

In the podcast "Where Does It Hurt?" Sales asks questions about how we develop theology or theologies that deal with a capitalist technocracy where only a few lives matter:

> We talk a lot today about black theologies but I want a liberating white theology. I want a theology that speaks to Appalachia. I want a theology that begins to deepen people's understanding of their capacity to live fully human lives and to touch the goodness inside of them rather than call upon the part of themselves that is not relational. Because it is nothing wrong with being European American. That is not the problem. It is how you actualize that history and how you actualize that reality.[6]

Sales's argument is that we need theology and theologies that raise all people from disposable pawns of a capitalist technocracy to "essentiality." And though it is fashionable to discuss marginalized nonwhite people who need liberation, there are masses of white people who have been excluded and marginalized as well and who equally stand in need of liberation. Sales is looking for a white theology that liberates and touches the goodness of people rather than fear and divisiveness.

Avoiding the demonization of all whites, she suggests that there is nothing wrong with being European American; the question is whether or not one performs white supremacy or whiteness with that history. Some European Americans work diligently to accept, affirm, and overcome the mistreatment of all marginalized people, excluded whites included, and live out a vision of freedom and justice for all. In my African American experience, I was deeply heartened that in response to the

---

5. Ruby Sales, "Where Does It Hurt?" The On Being Project, audio interview by Krista Tippett, https://www.youtube.com/watch?v=STa0KU6-4mw. Also quoted in Thomas, *How to Preach a Dangerous Sermon*, 10.

6. Ruby Sales, "Where Does It Hurt?"

May 25, 2020, murder of George Floyd, so many different people, not only in America, but all over the world, joined in solidarity with Black Lives Matter to march, protest, and in various other ways stand against institutional racism and police violence. What some have labeled as the "racial reckoning," was a multiracial movement of people who finally understood what Black people had been saying for generations about police violence and state-sanctioned terrorism in the policing of Black people. The God of the Dangerous Sermon does not demonize Euro-Americans or anyone else for that matter. The God of the Dangerous Sermon liberates and touches the goodness of people rather than instills fear and divisiveness, and that goodness raises people up from disposability to essentiality.

Too Much Forgiveness

Earlier, I quoted Harry S. Stout suggesting that African Americans were not complicit in slavery and were outside of the moral judgment by God of white Americans, as Lincoln outlined in the Second Inaugural.[7] Frederick Douglass was complimentary of the speech, but also had strong concerns and deep reservations. Standing outside of Lincoln's white audience, Douglass thought that too much forgiveness led to too much acceptance.[8] The acceptance of the South without punishment for insurrection would eventually mean re-enslavement for Black people by different means. As long as the nation's priority was preserving the Union, and not the racial equality that would preserve the Union, racism would endure and simply rear its ugly head in another form.

Of course, history has only proved Douglass right. As long as Washington kept troops in the South during the brief period of Reconstruction following the war, some progress toward racial equality was made. But it was short-lived. After those troops were removed via the Compromise of 1877, former slaves, left without federal protection, came under the

---

7. Stout, "Abraham Lincoln as Moral Leader," 84.

8. Stout, "Abraham Lincoln as Moral Leader," 84.

violence and intimidation of the Jim Crow era, which lasted well into the twentieth century. Douglass's fears were realized—that reconciliation without any kind of punishment would allow the South to revert to violently suppressing Blacks, and the North would acquiesce. Douglass said that after the government had asked the slave to "espouse the government's cause and turn against their masters, they were returned back to their masters without a single shred of protection."[9] In reality, the moral imagination of the majority of white Americans did not allow any real reconciliation between North and South without the re-subjugation of those who had been freed from bondage based in white racial pride and prejudice against people of color.

What is interesting and problematic at the same time is that though the North was complicit in slavery, and therefore the judgment of God, there was little remaking of the North in the image of racial equality. Of course, Lincoln did not live to further flesh out his vision of Reconstruction and any possibility of racial equality, and so the great moral paradox of white supremacy, even after more than six hundred thousand died in a civil war, lingered, reemerged in the form of Jim Crow, and has found this and other contemporary manners today to continue to infest the heart of American society.

The point at which white supremacy has most vehemently denied racial equality is what John Wilkes Booth earlier called "nigger citizenship." The threat of Black people with the right to fully participate in democracy by voting their interests has been at the heart of the fear and violence of white supremacy for centuries. The Voting Rights Act of 1965 was a landmark piece of federal legislation that prohibited racial discrimination in voting based in Jim Crow tactics and mob violence. It was designed to guarantee rights by the Fourteenth and Fifteenth Amendments long denied through violence, intimidation, and trickery of racial minorities, especially in the South. In 2013, the Supreme Court overturned the Voting Rights Act of 1965, in a 5-4 split, ruling that, given the evidence of the

---

9. Stout, "Abraham Lincoln as Moral Leader," 85.

election of a Black president, Barack Obama, the Voting Rights Act had achieved its main purpose.[10]

Fast forward to January 6, 2021, and the Capitol was overrun with insurrectionists who sought to overturn a duly elected president, Joseph R. Biden, in favor of, in essence, the autocratic monarchy of Donald J. Trump. Trump and many in the Republican Party convinced adherents of the "Big Lie" that the presidential election had been stolen from Trump. Conspiracy theories suggest the alleged theft was to have occurred in cities and counties that were primarily heavily concentrated with African American voters, such as Detroit, Atlanta, and Milwaukee, and, therefore, according to Trump and sympathizers, the election needed to be overturned. Despite factual evidence to the contrary, quite extensively proven in sixty court cases and numerous recounts that there had been no voter fraud, the Big Lie was propagated by Trump, conservative cable Fox News and other far-right media outlets, many Congressional Republicans, far-right social media platforms, and Trump voters. Quite naturally, their only conclusion was that the election had to be overturned, even if by violence. MSNBC commentator Joy Reid summed up perfectly my thoughts and feelings watching the mob violence of the Capitol:

> **White Americans are never afraid of the cops**, even when they're committing insurrection. Even when they're engaged in attempting to occupy our Capitol to steal the votes of people who look like me (black and brown people) because, in their minds, they own this country, they own that Capitol. They own the cops. The cops work for them, and people like me have no damn right to pick the president. . . . They get to pick the president,

---

10. Specifically, in *Shelby County v. Holder*, the Court overturned Section 4 of the Act, which laid out the formula for determining which states had to seek approval prior to enacting new voting laws. While Section 5 specifically addresses this requirement, the ruling on Section 4 renders Section 5 ineffective. Critics of the ruling, including Justice Ginsburg, argued that attempts to restrict minority voting in many southern states is still rampant, citing efforts in many states to redraw district maps in order to minimize the will of minorities. See "The Voting Rights Act of 1965 Overview," FindLaw, updated July 30, 2020, https://www.findlaw.com/voting/how-do-i-protect-my-right-to-vote-/the-voting-rights-act-of-1965-overview.html#:~:text=The%20Voting%20Rights%20Act%20of%201965%20was%20passed,found%20a%20key%20provision%20of%20the%20Act%20unconstitutional.

. . . if that was a Black Lives Matter protest in DC, there would already be people shackled, arrested, or dead en masse . . .[11]

Reid goes on to request that Alicia Garza, one of the founders of Black Lives Matter, be brought on the air. She would give witness to how Black Lives Matter marchers are treated at every turn—what it means and feels like to "protest" peacefully, unarmed, and get the wildly opposite treatment from what the insurrectionists on Capitol Hill received. The attempt to suppress the vote of millions in primarily African American cities and counties is another obvious attempt to suppress the Black vote. White supremacy fears the equality of the Black vote—Booth's "nigger citizenship."

Colin P. Clarke, in a January 22, 2021, *New York Times* op-ed, argues that the far-right extremism evidenced in the attempted Capitol insurrection will be long-lived.[12] He believes that the siege of the Capitol will be framed as a successful demonstration and, given the spread of images across social media platforms, will recruit MAGA (Make America Great Again) adherents. Though far-right extremists and white militias were heavily represented, large segments of the mob that stormed the Capitol were unaffiliated individuals, small groups, family members, neighbors. He considers these to be new foot soldiers for the extremist far right. Some have military experience or law enforcement training, and the infusion of young members will breathe new life into the movement, ensuring its longevity:

> Just as many Americans were motivated to join the U.S. military after the al Qaeda attacks of Sept. 11 in what they considered an act of patriotism, some may now enlist in anti-government militias or racially motivated extremist groups in an act of reverse patriotism. . . . Jan. 6 will be just as symbolic for far right extremists as the date Sept. 11 is to Americans.[13]

---

11. Emma Nolan, "Joy Reid Says BLM Protesters Would Be 'Shackled, Arrested or Dead' in Viral Speech on Race," *Newsweek*, January 7, 2021, https://www.newsweek.com/joy-reid-blm-protesters-shackled-arrested-dead-viral-speech-race-1559759.

12. Colin P. Clarke, "A New Era of Far Right Violence," *The New York Times*, January 22, 2021, https://www.nytimes.com/2021/01/22/opinion/domestic-terrorism-far-right-insurrection.html.

13. Clarke, "A New Era of Far Right Violence."

According to Clarke, following a PBS NewsHour Marist poll, 8 percent of Americans surveyed said they supported the insurrection. He reasoned that the turbulence of the next years should not be underestimated. He says "record-setting firearm sales, looming economic calamity, continued fraying of America's social fabric, exacerbated by declining mental health, rising domestic violence and worsening substance abuse—make for . . . the potential for race and ethnically based violence."[14] Again, white supremacist violence against Black and brown people for simply attempting to be citizens. Eternal vigilance against white supremacy and white nationalism and my right, and the right of many others, to be a human being and citizen will be my cause until the day that I meet my maker.

I was once giving a public lecture, and in the question-and-answer section, a young seminarian asked me about my statement that white supremacy and white nationalism can never be reasoned with, that it and its adherents must be walled off and defeated. For him, my language was un-Christian and unforgiving, and he argued that it was my Christian duty to reconcile. I asked him how it is possible to reconcile with people who believe and operate in conspiracy theories, denial of facts, and alternate realities? How can one reason with people who believe that the election was stolen, even in the face of all rational evidence and substantiated logical facts, with sixty unsuccessful challenges in court of voter fraud? In the face of all this, estimates are that 70 percent of Republicans and 60 percent of self-identified conservatives still believe that Joe Biden stole the election. The Big Lie of a stolen election has been repeated relentlessly by Trump and his enablers, including 147 Republican lawmakers who challenged the electoral college results on the same day hours after the mob of insurrectionists stormed the Capitol. I did not retreat then, and I do not retreat now. I do not advocate violence or hate, but people who are immune to reason cannot be reasoned with. They must be walled off so they can do as little harm as possible.

There is a tremendous amount of discussion about moving forward toward healing and unity, particularly by Republican elected officials.

14. Clarke, "A New Era of Far Right Violence."

Let me say this unequivocally: there can be no reconciliation and healing without accountability. Those who perpetrated the Big Lie must stand in front of the American people, and especially their Republican base, and say, "The Big Lie is indeed a lie and Joseph Biden won the election fair and square." How can you build healing and unity when a lie of this magnitude and viciousness still pervades the American landscape? I want to be clear, I believe in forgiveness and I also believe that racism and those who act out their Euro-American history in white supremacist terms must be walled off and defeated—whether they be insurrectionists doing mob violence, or dignified legislative leaders in tailored suits who support voter suppression. They must be out-voted despite voter suppression and all of the allegations of voter fraud that masquerade as an attempt to disenfranchise Black and brown people. Again, when you endorse the Big Lie, you cannot possibly be serving a universal God.

I wholeheartedly agree with this sentiment expressed by Frederick Douglass: "I would unite with anybody to do right and with nobody to do wrong." I cannot get past the Big Lie because it is connected to the biggest of lies, started in the 1400s with the racial paradigm: that white people are superior and are the only "real" Americans. There can be no reconciliation without truth.

Your Little Finger

Gun culture in America, when compared to other nations of the world, is distinctively shaped by the large number of guns owned by civilians (more than 300 million), generally permissive regulations, and high levels of gun violence. Gun ownership is protected by the right to bear arms in the Second Amendment of the Constitution. Firearms are used for self-defense, hunting, and recreation, such as target shooting. In Sondheim's "Gun Song" from his Broadway musical *Assassins*, the gun is used for political violence, that is, the shooting and killing of someone because of disagreement with their political or moral position. Sondheim puts these words in the mouth of John Wilkes Booth, Lincoln's assassin, saying that all one has to do is:

> Move your little finger and—
> You can change the world.[15]

Booth sought to change political dynamics and history by the assassination of Lincoln, and that he very much did. His action and similar assassinations, such as those of Martin Luther King Jr. and others in America and around the world, by guns and other means, begs the question of whether violence has the power to continually thwart movements of those who aspire to freedom, liberation, and equality. In American history, the movement against white supremacy and for freedom and justice has been perennially threatened by violence and killing, including lynching, bombings, brutality, intimidation, mob violence, rape, blackmail, and murder, often without consequence and accountability. This is the question of power and whether or not the power of hate, violence, and murder can overcome love, truth, and justice. This question speaks to my belief in the gospel of Jesus Christ.

At the heart of my working gospel is not only the teaching of the prophetic messiah, but his actual murder, lynching, and death at Calvary. He was arrested, beaten, tortured, and killed by crucifixion at the hand of the state, the result of religious and political bigotry and instigated mob sentiment, and it looked like weakness and being vanquished. It looked like Jesus's movement on behalf of the universal God was stopped, and love, truth, and justice were defeated. And yet the resurrection is the evidence and guarantor that hate, lies, and violence will never ultimately win. As Paul says in 2 Corinthians 13:4, "Certainly he was crucified in weakness, but he lives by the power of God." The resurrection is the demonstration of the victory of God's weakness over human strength as 1 Corinthians 1:22–25 (NRSV) states:

---

15. Stephen Sondheim, "Gun Song," http://www.songlyrics.com/stephen-sondheim/gun-song -lyrics/.

> For Jews demand signs and Greeks desire wisdom, but we proclaim Christ
> crucified, a stumbling block to Jews and foolishness to Gentiles, but to
> those who are the called, both Jews and Greeks, Christ the power of God
> and the wisdom of God. For God's foolishness is wiser than human wis-
> dom, and God's weakness is stronger than human strength.

The resurrection reveals that divine goodness overcomes the power of the
world with what the world regards as weakness. In Jesus, the prophetic
Messiah, God turns weakness into strength by death on a cross. This is the
great mystery of our faith—death is swallowed up in victory and strength
is made perfect in weakness. Hate, violence, intimidation, lynching, assassination, and even death itself is overcome in the resurrection of Jesus
Christ.

Our purpose herein is to respond to the question of why so few have
and so many have not. Earlier I suggested that dominant classes at the top
of the moral hierarchy based their economic interests in attempts to maintain their privilege in all aspects of society, often bending government and
culture to their will. What does this aforementioned divine mystery of the
resurrection of the prophetic Messiah mean in the economic and political arena where so much of the actual division of resources is based upon
elections? The work of Stacey Abrams and many grassroot organizations
represents a form of gospel-inspired hope that can defeat the cynicism and
despair of white supremacy and white nationalism.

Stacey Abrams gave a closing speech in her unsuccessful run for governor of Georgia on November 16, 2018, that has proven to be a significant marker for government working for all of the people. Her successful
opponent, Brian Kemp, as secretary of state attempted to prevent tens of
thousands of registered voters from casting ballots, including a large and
disproportionate number of African Americans. Kemp won the race with
50.22 percent of the vote. Abrams then gave a speech to her supporters the
night of the announcement of Kemp's victory.

The speech communicated powerful themes concerning democracy
and asked Kemp to ignore calls to make voting even more difficult in
communities of color. She said that when some notice voter engagement
in communities of color, they invent claims of fraud or lie about the cost

of democracy in justification of closing more polling places and stifling the vote of people of color. Though she acknowledged that Kemp would be certified as victor, she could not concede based upon the level of "incompetence and mismanagement" that called into serious question election integrity in Georgia:

> *Make no mistake, the former Secretary of State was deliberate and intentional in his actions. I know that eight years of systemic disenfranchisement, disinvestment and incompetence had its desired effect on the electoral process in Georgia . . . I know that millions of Georgians, of Americans—of goodwill and various partisan beliefs—are enraged by these truths. In response, you may seek to vent your anger, or worse, turn away from politics because it can be as rigged and rotten as you've always believed. I implore each of you to not give in to that* anger or apathy but instead turn to action. Because the antidote to injustice is progress. The cure to this malpractice is a fight for fairness in every election held—in every law passed—in every decision made.[16]

Like poll taxes and literacy tests of the Jim Crow era, modern voter suppression efforts are relentless and effective, but Abrams would not leave the resolution of this unfairness to cynicism, despair, and violence and announced the launch of Fair Fight Georgia to pursue accountability in Georgia's elections and integrity in maintaining voting rolls. She committed to channeling the work of her campaign into a strong legal demand for reform of elections in Georgia and committed to working across party lines to find a common purpose in protecting democracy, and registering people to vote.

Most experts agree that Stacey Abrams and Fair Fight, along with other grassroots organizations and activists, were decisive in turning Georgia to the Democratic presidential candidate in 2020 and also to winning the Democratic Senate seats for Jon Ossoff and Raphael Warnock. Abrams commented that the road to victory was long, with 10 million door knocks, millions of texts and phone calls, and still more work to be done.

On the heels of these Georgia victories, it is clear that Georgia Republicans will push new voting regulations. It seems that Republican

---

16. Heather Timmons, "Stacey Abrams' concession speech is a powerful critique of US civil rights," Quartz Media, November 19, 2018, https://qz.com/1468560/read-stacey-abrams-full-concession-speech/.

legislators across the country are preparing a slew of new voting restrictions in lieu of President Trump's loss, with Georgia as the focal point. Republicans are citing the Big Lie as the reason for declining trust in election integrity by their constituencies and as an excuse for the restrictions. Senator Larry Walker, the vice chair of the Republican Senate Caucus, said his constituents were deeply concerned, saying he has received thousands of emails, letters, and texts: "A large percentage of my constituents have lost faith in the integrity of our election system. So we are going to try to address something that we feel like can restore the public's confidence."[17] If Walker's constituency has lost faith in the integrity in elections, it is because of the Big Lie that Trump and Republicans fostered in their echo chamber and constituencies. Rather than go to work as Abrams did in the face of defeat to convince voters of their ideas and programs, they seek voter suppression tactics to limit minority voting by changing the rules. Some Republicans have been blunt, as was Trump, in saying Republicans cannot win unless they change the rules. In voting surveys before the 2020 presidential elections, around three-quarters of Americans favored requiring all voters to show government-issued photo identification to vote, though voter IDs disproportionately affect minority voters. Will we be willing to allow them to limit the access of Black and brown constituencies—or that of any voting base that is not Republican—to vote?

There are many like Stacey Abrams around America who work for freedom, justice, and eradication of voter suppression and systemic racism. My argument is that faith in the death, burial, and resurrection of Jesus Christ gives us the confidence and power to fight in and for fairness rather than resort to cynicism, apathy, despair, and its concomitants, manipulation, violence, and intimidation. I am encouraged by how much justice work is going on. Political action is needed, in the manner of Stacey Abrams, William Barber, and many others who use their faith to upend the powers of white supremacy and provide moral imagination outside the 1400s racial paradigm.

---

17. Zach Montellaro, "State Republicans push new voting restrictions after Trump's loss," *Politico*, January 24, 2021, https://www.politico.com/news/2021/01/24/republicans-voter-id-laws-461707.

Moral Imagination Outside the Racial Paradigm

After a clear and thorough summation, David Fitch, in "Shall We Go Be Among the Oppressed?" raises critical questions in light of James Cone's critique of Reinhold Niebuhr.[18] Fitch comments that, after reading Cone, the temptation is to adopt Niebuhr's Christian realism and engage in battles of pitting one coercive power over another, the tactics of injustice in the attempt to overcome injustice. According to Fitch, Cone leads readers to default to the Niebuhrian option. Must liberation theology engage the violence of the world on the world's own violent terms to end and overcome violence?

Fitch argues that evangelicals are Niebuhrians. Power is seen as the only way, whether involving government, church, special interests, local and national politics, or structural issues related to local and national politics. The struggle against abortion, sexism, or racism, for example, must exclusively be framed as power against power. The justification is: this is how the world works and we must deal with the world as it is. Justice work must be done on the world's terms. Fitch says we enter these power struggles on the world's terms and push for righteousness as God gives Christians the ability to see it, but here is what's wrong with this approach:

> [T]his not only ends up putting the onus on our activism to make things work, it postures us as *coercive* in the world. This . . . produces both the evangelical Right and the progressive evangelical Left's posture in the world.
> . . . [E]ntering the world on the world's terms, using the world's power to defeat that same power, *replicates the structures of that power*. It perpetuates oppression in unpredictable directions.[19]

---

18. David Fitch, "Shall We Go Be Among the Oppressed? Reflections on James Cone's 'The Cross and the Lynching Tree,' (Part I)," Missio Alliance, April 10, 2018, https://www.missioalliance.org/shall-we-go-be-among-the-oppressed-reflections-on-james-cones-the-cross-and-the-lynching-tree-part-1/, and Fitch, "Shall We Go Be Among the Oppressed? . . . (Part 2)," April 11, 2018, https://www.missioalliance.org/shall-we-go-be-among-the-oppressed-james-cones-the-cross-and-the-lynching-tree-part-2/.

19. Fitch, "Shall We Go Be Among the Oppressed? . . . (Part 1)."

This is the trap that, most recently and visibly, white Christian evangelicals and other Christians fell into in their support of Trump. The agreement was that Trump would carry the white Christian evangelical agenda and they would vote for him and keep quiet as Trump did whatever was necessary to accomplish the agenda and anything else that he wanted to do. Trump used coercion to foster white evangelical causes and other white supremacist goals and consequences, such as separating immigrant families and putting children in cages at the border. Based upon the agreement, white and other Christian supporters of Trump were basically silent at these and other measures such as the Muslim ban. The consequence of Christian silence was the sacrificing of Christian morals and witness, and such costs grew higher and higher right up to the Capitol insurrection. Many thought that might finally be the breaking point, but the insurrection lost Trump very little white evangelical Christian support. This is the result of Christians singularly relying upon the world's power to fulfill an understanding of Christian agenda.

While I concur with Fitch's overall point as regards the temptation of using the world's power, Cone's extensive treatment of Martin Luther King Jr. offers, from the Black religious tradition, an alternative to Niebuhr. Cone says: "King had a different take on love and justice because he spoke to and for whose faith, focused on the cross of Jesus, mysteriously empowered them to fight against impossible odds."[20] Cone suggests that King never spoke of proximate justice or about what was practically possible to achieve, because it would have killed the revolutionary spirit of the movement. Cone recounts that King would call out before a demonstration, "What do you want?" "Freedom!" the demonstrators would shout back, ready to face angry white mobs, policemen, and dogs. King would ask, "When do you want it?" "Now" was the resounding response, as protestors would begin walking and singing together, "Ain't Gonna Let Nobody Turn Me Around."[21] This created a revolutionary spirit that sent people into the streets prepared to shoulder the cross, ready to meet whatever fate at the hands of mobs, violence, or the state-sanctioned terrorism of the

---

20. Cone, *The Cross and the Lynching Tree*, 72.

21. Cone, *The Cross and the Lynching Tree*, 72.

police. There was not any talk of proximate justice, a little bit of justice that whites dole out to Blacks to keep the racial paradigm in place. Cone suggests the Black church in its faith in the death and resurrection of Jesus and the power of the Spirit of God as an alternative to Neibuhr's concept of power. Cone sourced this religious tradition of the Black church as the "God of the Oppressed," or in my words, the God of the Dangerous Sermon.

The deepest theological reflection that Fitch pushes us to in raising the question of whether there is any other method than the coercive violence of the world is, in my words, "Is there any moral imagination for human community outside of the 1400s racial paradigm?"

Brandin Francabandera critiques Niebuhr and my development of rhetorical theology as well: "Social analysis seems to be the driving force of his work and theology is used only if it can buttress the argumentation of that analysis—if it is used at all."[22] Francabandera points out that, when Niebuhr defines religion as individual morality and "a sense of the absolute," he:

> fails to speak of the *church* specifically as a collective life, which is enabled to live by the power of the spirit. This lack of detailed ecclesiology weakens Niebuhr's argument as it applies directly to the Christian collective life. If it can be argued that the church embodies an alternative politic and is called to live collectively as a witness to all other politics, then Niebuhr's point here seems to be damaged to some degree. That is to say, the church stands as a witness of collective life rightly lived, and in this way judges all other politics of society. In speaking of the inevitability of injustice and collective life, Niebuhr runs the risk of damaging this aspect of the church's witness.[23]

In many cases, the church is exactly what Niebuhr says it is, idolatry that allows people to be individually good and then participate in some of the most painful and devastating hypocrisy and evil. I take Fitch to say that Niebuhr does not go far enough to construct a vision of Christian

---

22. Brandin Francabandera, "Review of *Moral Man and Immoral Society* by Reinhold Niebuhr" (February 2016), Blogegesis, https://brandinfranca.wordpress.com/2016/03/01/review-of-moral-man-and-immoral-society-by-reinhold-niebuhr/.

23. Francabandera, "Review of *Moral Man and Immoral Society* by Reinhold Niebuhr."

community that challenges and critiques the separation between individual goodness and group sin and violence. What would be a vision of ecclesiology that, in Niebuhrian terms, allows believers to transcend self-interest and self-deception both individually and collectively and repent on both fronts, fostering love, justice, and mercy? The Black church has surely not reached these heights, but occasionally, in the best of the African American church and preaching tradition, we have reached toward these heights and showed the world an alternative to the global racial paradigm—hence, I seek to do and be the best of the tradition and serve the God of the Dangerous Sermon.

The God of the Dangerous Sermon by the power of the Spirit, as Fitch says, "moves people and systems towards redemption, reconciliation, forgiveness, healing, cooperation, and transformation" both personal and social.[24] The God of the Dangerous Sermon is against, is the opposite of, and confronts the tribal God of violence and coercion, not on the world's terms of cynicism, hate, and intimidation, but with the power of vulnerability, love, and redemption based in the death and resurrection of Jesus Christ. The resurrected Christ presents a healing way forward in the formation of a new reconciled community that overcomes the global racial paradigm and all efforts to harm, maim, oppress, or violate human beings, individually or through systems. God has defeated evil in the world, brought principalities and power to their knees, and overcome the chains of sin and antagonism through the death, burial, resurrection, and exaltation of Jesus.

Outside of the power of the Spirit of God, I do not believe that much of the church has the moral imagination to reach the heights and depths of Christian ecclesiology that is required of us as Christians to play a role in challenging and transforming this culture of white supremacy and its place deep in the heart of the citadel of American culture. At best, many churches send volunteers into the world to do the work of justice as what Fitch calls, "training organizations." This is good, and we win skirmishes in the battle for justice, but we never get to the place for the *renewal of all things in Christ* because only true Christian community can renew all

---

24. Fitch, "Shall We Go Be Among the Oppressed? (Part 2)."

things. Imagine the level of community that we would have to live at as Christians to renew all things for Christ. When we engage the world's violence with more violence, we strengthen the tribal God of intimidation, racism, gender violence, homophobia, voter suppression, violence, insurrection, lynching, mass incarceration, and other evils. Not only do we add more violence to the world, but we miss our deepest calling as the church of Jesus Christ.

When have we seen this kind of church? Fitch recounts stories of the early civil rights movement in the southern United States:

> It was Charles Sherrod and those early Student Non-Violent Coordinating Committee (SNCC) meetings that had multi-racial prayer meetings and sit-ins of presence on southern campuses and town centers that disrupted the ensconced Jim Crow society of the South. Sherrod said that it was the "reconciliation that occurs within the Christian community (that) is the deepest and most permanent of reconciliations." . . . [R]econciliation is a deep practice of God's victorious presence in the world.[25]

The goal was radical Christian community rather than simply gaining power over the oppressors.

Another example is the aforementioned Clarence Jordan, farmer and New Testament scholar, whom we referenced earlier. Of course, I am not suggesting that everyone needs to live communally, sharing material possessions, but I am suggesting radical Christian community. Radical Christian community and the rhetorical construction of the God of the Dangerous Sermon allow for adherents to see, acknowledge, and recognize the full humanity of anyone outside of their group. Therefore they are not easily susceptible to stereotypes, hate, conspiracy theories, oppression, and the demonization of people. They are loyal to the universal God of all humanity, the God of peace and justice who offers healing and judgment to all individuals and nations. The God of the Dangerous Sermon and of radical Christian community offers enemies redemption, redeems the god of war and conquest, and never guarantees that enemies will be destroyed and one people or nation will be given domination, generation

---

25. Fitch, "Shall We Go Be Among the Oppressed? (Part 2)."

upon generation. The God of the Dangerous Sermon is a universal, never a nationalist God.

I close the chapter with words of Clarence Jordan that represent for me the God of the Dangerous Sermon:

> God will seek us—how long? Until he finds us. And when he's found the last little shriveling rebellious soul and has depopulated hell, then death will be swallowed up in victory, and Christ will turn over all things to the Father that he may be all and in all. Then every tongue shall confess that Jesus Christ is Lord, to the glory of God the Father.[26]

26. Clarence Jordan "God's Destination for Man," in *The Substance of Faith: And Other Cotton Patch Sermons*, ed. Dallas Lee (Koinonia Partners, 2005), 169–70.

The resurrection of Jesus was simply God's unwillingness to take our "no" for an answer. He raised Jesus, not as an invitation to us to come to heaven when we die, but as a declaration that he himself has now established permanent, eternal residence here on earth. He is standing beside us, strengthening us in this life. The good news of the resurrection of Jesus is not that we shall die and go home to be with him, but that he has risen and comes home with us, bringing all his hungry, naked, thirsty, sick prisoner brothers with him.

—Clarence Jordan

Rhetorical theology is a contextual enterprise and locates itself in the reality that some have so much and others have so little. Following the Prophetic Messiah of Luke 4, I believe the universal God, while caring for all humankind, slants concern particularly towards the poor, captive, imprisoned, and oppressed. Rhetoric allows us to ascertain the God to whom the speaker is appealing based upon what the speaker calls the audience to do and be. As my colleague at Christian Theological Seminary, Rob Saler, suggests, "all God talk is not equal." All religion is not inherently good. Rhetorical theology helps to discern if the speaker is serving a tribal or universal God.

The Bible reminds us in Matthew 7:1 not to judge others, lest we be judged. We often interpret this verse to mean a lack of tolerance of any judgment, and therefore the acceptance of many morally questionable behaviors lest we be seen as critical, judgmental, and arrogant. But there are times when so much is at stake in the moral arena that we must use our best moral discernment and judgment and take a position as to what is right and wrong, acceptable and unacceptable behavior, good and bad religion. I

153

am critical of white Christian evangelicals based upon the bargain that they struck with former president Donald Trump. Many seem enamored with Trump's style of aggression, attack, and whatever else it takes to defeat the enemy of the "radical left." They have ignored morality and common decency in their interest of garnering a federal judiciary, tax cuts, lack of tolerance for abortion, restrictive immigration, and a return to the idyllic dream of a white Christian America. Nothing Trump has done or can do, even inciting an insurrection to overtake the Capitol, seems to diminish their support. Trump famously said that he could shoot someone in the middle of Fifth Avenue and not lose support, and Christians comprise part of his base that makes that statement plausible and true. From the perspective of white Christians following Trump they have gained much.

But at what cost? First, how can they ever again credibly make arguments of how much moral character matters when their glaring hypocrisy in support of Trump has stripped them of any moral authority? Second, what distinctive Christian behavior have evangelical Christians brought to politics? They have become no better than any other secular lobby or interest group that plays power politics to achieve their ends. Third, they have inflicted tremendous damage on the overall Christian witness in America. As the Trump brand they support has been self-righteous, judgmental, angry, arrogant, petty, racist, vindictive, always victimized, and ungracious, so must be the (tribal) god that they proclaim despite their quoting of Christian scriptures. The public is looking for dialogical religion and a god that is consistent with the essential parts of true dialogue, including self-critique, transparency, accountability, and honesty about the construction of authority. In white evangelical support of Trump and white Christian nationalism, the Christian faith is not dialogical.

While this description is not indicative of all white evangelicals,[1] it seems to fit the overwhelming majority who have supported Trump. They surely have legitimate concerns that need to be heard and resolved, but the

---

1. Following the January 6, 2021, attack on the Capitol, growing movements of Christians began to break from traditional evangelical churches such as the Southern Baptist Church (SBC) and to call for Christian nationalism to be condemned and denounced as heresy. See Christians against Christian Nationalism, christiansagainstchristiannationalism.org; and Charlie Dates, "'We Out': Charlie Dates on why his church is leaving the SBC over rejection of critical race theory," Religion News Service, December 18, 2020, https://religionnews.com/2020/12/18/we-out-charlie-dates-on-why-his-church-is-leaving-the-sbc-over-rejection-of-critical-race-theory/.

bottom line is that they have gained access to power and influence at the expense of the gospel that they proclaim. The long and painful cultural history of this country, following the global racial paradigm of the 1400s European conquest and theft, has shown much of white America to be serving the tribal capitalistic God of white supremacy. And the majority of white evangelicals, along with some Christians in the Roman Catholic and Black churches, have gone right along with American culture.

Some will say that I have been un-Christian. I am not foolish enough to pretend that I am beyond critique, but silence was not an option for me in this critical time. Martin Luther King Jr. said on the night of his "Beyond Vietnam" speech, when he took a position against the Vietnam War: "A time comes when silence is betrayal. . . . And some of us who have already begun to break the silence of the night have found that the calling to speak is often a vocation of agony, but we must speak. We must speak with all the humility that is appropriate to our limited vision, but we must speak."[2] Realizing my limited vision, I must say this: in the sweep of the long history of white supremacy since the 1400s, consistent historically with the majority of the white church in America, white evangelicals and Christians who support Trump are serving a tribal God.

Thank God white evangelicalism is not the entirety of Christianity in America. Thank God Christianity maintains a global witness the world over and a very different evangelicalism is growing significantly in many parts of the world, which the fecklessness of the American white evangelical church cannot diminish. Thank God for the strong pockets of renewal, even from the beginning of the Trump era, inside white evangelicalism where people were/are willing to move past white supremacy to the mandates of the universal God.

Like Lincoln, quoting scripture in his Second Inaugural Address, I say woe to those leaders of the Trump era who have led the people astray:

But whosoever shall offend one of these little ones which believe in me, it were better for him that a millstone were hanged about his neck. . . . Woe

---

2. Martin Luther King Jr., "Beyond Vietnam—A Time to Break Silence," American Rhetoric, April 4, 1967, https://www.americanrhetoric.com/speeches/mlkatimetobreaksilence.htm.

unto the world because of offenses! . . . woe to the man by whom the offense cometh! (Matthew 18:6–7 KJV)

Woe, indeed, to the leaders who have led the people astray with the continuation of the original lie with the Big Lie. In each book of my Dangerous Sermon series, I have quoted this from T. S. Eliot:

> The number of people in possession of any criteria for discriminating between good and evil is very small . . . the number of the half-alive hungry for any form of spiritual experience, or for what offers itself as spiritual experience, high or low, good or bad, is considerable. My own generation has not served them very well. . . . Woe to the foolish prophets that . . . have seen nothing![3]

The number of people who have thought through deeply, profoundly, and carefully their moral values, and therefore are able to discriminate between good and evil, is very small. Too many Americans, regardless of the facts, blindly follow the opinion of leaders. For far too many, their trusted tribal leaders establish "truth"—what is right and wrong and who is friend and enemy. Good is what my leader and group do and evil is what the other side does, regardless of the moral merits of behavior. People are hungry for some form of spiritual experience, or what offers itself as spiritual experience whether it is the high universal or low tribal dream, morally good or bad. Woe unto those who have seen nothing and yet lead people astray. Those who have led the people into moral decay will receive a difficult judgment from God.

Throughout this book, I have advocated eternal vigilance against white supremacy. White supremacy continues as I breathe the very air it takes to write these words. Keishan N. Blain said this to describe the reality that Black and brown people deal with every day:

> The invasion of the Capitol on January 6 connects to a long history of white supremacist violence and terror. Throughout the nation's history, white people have often used violence and intimidation to retain power— the list is long and includes white militias in the Antebellum South, the

---

3. T. S. Eliot, *After Strange Gods: A Primer of Modern Heresy; The Page-Barbour Lectures at the University of Virginia, 1933* (London: Faber and Faber 1934; reprint, Forgotten Books, 2018).

rise of the Ku Klux Klan after the Civil War and the Wilmington massacre of 1898. The insurrection of January 6 is only the most recent iteration of white supremacist violence cloaked under the guise of "political dissent." The presence of racist symbols such as the Confederate flag and the noose underscore this point.[4]

Deep in the bowels of the best of the religious traditions of Black people in America is the admonition not to hate, but to love. One of my friends, pastor Johnny Ray Youngblood, tells the story of growing up and not being allowed to use four-letter words. At the top of the list was this four-letter word: h-a-t-e. I was raised not to hate anyone. Clarence Jordan helped me to learn to have compassion. The Koinonia Farm community was put out of the local Baptist church. Jordan describes what happens, and at the end of it he says about the church people:

> I tell you that not to reflect bad or evil on anyone except to show you the tremendous struggle going on in the hearts of southern people. I don't think they are vicious devils. I think they are people with the good and the evil and it's pulling against them. There is this struggle between an ideal and a tradition that exerts a tremendous pull in their lives. They want to do what they know Christ teaches and yet they are not strong enough to break with the traditions in which they found themselves.[5]

Following the Scriptures, Clarence Jordan said that we must overcome evil with good.

I close by updating and paraphrasing King's famous words that he has made the decision to love because love is ultimately the only solution for humankind:

> I have seen too much to hate. I've seen too much hate on the faces of too many insurrectionists who ravaged the Capitol. I've seen hate on the faces of too many Proud Boys and Boogaloo Bois to want to hate, myself, because every time I see it, I know it does something to their faces and personalities,

4. "This Acquittal Sends Three Dangerous Messages to Future Presidents," Politico, February 13, 2021, https://www.politico.com/news/magazine/2021/02/13/impeachment-vote-history-roundup -468998.

5. Clarence Jordon tells the Koinonia story, https://www.youtube.com/watch?v=2g1Z-v-TpI0 &t=2186s.

and I say to myself that hate is too great a burden to bear. I have decided to love.[6]

My decision to love does not mean I will not oppose white supremacy with every nonviolent fiber of my being. Love is not emotional bosh, but a creative and powerful force for what is good, lovely, and true in the world, the oncoming of God's realm.

6. Paraphrased from Martin Luther King Jr., "Where Do We Go from Here?" Annual report delivered at the 11th Convention of the Southern Christian Leadership Conference, August 16, 1967, Atlanta, GA (Excerpts), http://www-personal.umich.edu/~gmarkus/MLK_WhereDoWeGo.pdf.